Research on Language and Social Interaction

VOLUME 29, NUMBER 1 – 1996

Table of Contents

Partings: Stuart Sigman et al.

Several members of the editorial board who have been associated with this journal as long as I have served as editor — since 1987 — are stepping down. Vern Cronen, Michael Moerman, Barnett Pearce, and Rod Watson are each leaders in the community this journal serves who have been willing to take on the additional burden of helping with editorial decisions and providing colleagues with feedback. I want to take this opportunity to publicly acknowledge their important contribution to the journal's quality and evolution and to thank them.

Stuart Sigman is also stepping down as the journal's associate editor, and he deserves a special salute. Stuart was the one who started the journal on its current path. He was invited by the publisher of *Papers in Linguistics* in 1985 to edit a special issue. In the process, he not only ended up with a double issue, but recast the journal and retitled it *Research on Language and Social Interaction*. At that point he decided to turn down an invitation to continue as editor, got me involved, and stayed on to serve as Associate Editor on Volumes 22 through 28. He has been a valued colleague, working with me on editorial policy, and taking on the essential chore of making the journal known and visible across disciplinary boundaries, and attracting submissions. We all owe it to him that we have this journal at all, and he deserves special credit for having the original vision of the journal's mission and community. I personally owe him in addition the collaborative support and advice he has generously given. Although his official role on the journal has ended, I will certainly continue to consult him as I have in the past, on those occasions when our two heads are better than my one.

Robert E. Sanders, Editor
Department of Communication
University at Albany, SUNY

Acknowledgment

We are indebted to the following reviewer–consultants for their help in the 1994–95 academic year.

Guest Reviewers

Janet Bavelas, *University of Victoria*
Wayne Beach, *San Diego State University*
Donal Carbaugh, *University of Massachusetts at Amherst*
Steven Clayman, *UCLA*
Kent Drummond, *University of Wyoming*
Jean Berko Gleason, *Boston University*
Patrick Gonzales, *UCLA*
Margorie Harness Goodwin, *University of South Carolina*
William Gudykunst, *California State University-Fullerton*
Joan Kelly Hall, *University of Georgia*
Christine Iacobucci, *Ithaca College*
Scott Jacobs, *University of Arizona*
Sally Jacoby, *UCLA*

Young Yun Kim, *University of Oklahoma*
Joachim Knuf, *University of Kentucky*
Edward Lamoureux, *Bradley University*
Jenny Mandelbaum, *Rutgers University*
Douglas Maynard, *Indiana University*
Robert Nofsinger, *Washington State University*
Brian Spitzberg, *San Diego State University*
Jurgen Streeck, *University of Texas at Austin*
Carolyn Taylor, *University of Illinois*
Anita Vangelisti, *University of Texas at Austin*
Julie Yingling, *Humboldt State University*

Research on Language and Social Interaction, 29(1), 1–5

Constituting Gender Through Talk in Childhood: Conversations in Parent–Child, Peer, and Sibling Relationships

Amy Sheldon
Department of Speech-Communication
University of Minnesota

This issue of *Research on Language and Social Interaction* explores some of the ways in which gender, as a social construction, might be rooted in and contingent on conversational processes in childhood. The interconnections between language and gender in three key developmental sociolinguistic contexts are examined: talk between parent and child (Ely et al., Reese et al.), talk among friends (Sheldon), and talk between siblings (DeHart).

When children learn to speak a language, they also learn to use it in ways that can reflect, resist, or ignore their culture's norms of acceptable feminine and masculine behavior. The authors of these articles explore the concept of talk as a medium in which both young children and the adults in their world "do" gender.

FORMATIVE INFLUENCES

The focus placed on adult talk by prevailing research in language and gender is here shifted to the study of talk in early childhood

Correspondence concerning this article should be sent to Amy Sheldon, Department of Speech-Communication, 460 Folwell Hall, University of Minnesota, 9 Pleasant Street, SE, Minneapolis, MN 55455. E-mail: asheldon@maroon.tc.umn.edu

contexts, the formative influences on adults' gendered language interaction. The children studied here range in age from 2 years to almost 6
years. The types of discourses studied include children's conversations
during pretend play construction and role play (DeHart, Sheldon),
parent and child reports of past speech (Ely et al.), parent and child
reminiscences of past events (Reese et al.), and children's persuasive
justifications and the negotiation of disagreements (DeHart, Sheldon).
These articles also underscore the collaborative aspect of the contexts in
which children develop what are often thought of as individual achieve-
ments: for example, memory of past events, reasoning skills, knowledge
of the world, conflict management and self-assertion skills, imagination, and so on.

Whereas we take for granted the role that adults have in socializing
children, the articles by Ely et al. and Reese et al., in particular, detail
how language is used by mothers and fathers, often to treat girls and
boys differently. The Ely et al. article considers how gender affects the
emphasis a speaker places on reporting speech events. The Reese et al.
article explores the bidirectional influences between parent and child.
They consider the child's role in shaping interactions with adults; girls
and boys elicit different adult responses when they talk about past
events.

Clearly, this collection of articles indicates that the study of talk
must be sensitive to differences in context: for example, setting, topic,
activity, and most importantly, who one's partner is. In addition, the
authors demonstrate how children themselves are active contributors to
the social construction of gender and the appearance (or nonappear-
ance) of gender differences in discourse (see especially the articles by
Reese et al. and Sheldon).

COMPARISON AND CONTEXT

The juxtaposition of parent–child talk, peer talk, and sibling talk in
this issue is intended to model a comparative framework for language
and gender research. A comparative approach can help to avoid facile
overgeneralizations about gender differences in language-in-use, which

treat discourse as a context-free phenomenon. It can yield a much fuller understanding of how the context of talk shapes what is said to a large extent, and correlates with what has been called "gendered" language. It can yield a better understanding of how gendered talk reflects a speaker's responsiveness to the sociolinguistic features of the discourse context and the behavioral norms that are operating. This journal issue underscores the need to problematize the study of language and gender, a subfield of sociolinguistics, as the context-sensitive study of language-in-use.

The idea that gendered talk is situationally dependent is not new (e.g., see discussions by Goodwin, 1980; Thorne, 1986; and Sheldon, 1990, 1992). At the root of concern with how context affects the gendering of talk is the following question: When we describe gender differences in language use, are we actually confounding gender with situation? Whereas two of the articles in this collection experimentally manipulate context (Ely et al. and Reese et al.), the juxtaposition of all four of these studies also articulates a concern with context. The contrast between DeHart's article and the others in this collection, especially, highlights the importance of studying language and gender comparatively. DeHart extended research on peer talk to the sibling context and did not find differences noted previously in peer talk research. Her work suggests that siblings, because of the permanence and intimacy of their relationship, operate with greater freedom from gender-based interactional constraints. Sibling discourse emerges here as a key context for testing the generalizability of claims about language and gender and for probing whether research to date has confounded gender with situation. The Reese et al. article is a different kind of example of how being sensitive to the effect of situation on discourse can bear fruit.

Another way to think about context is modeled by the Sheldon article and the conversation analytic tradition it rests on. "Context" here is prior text. Close analysis of text describes how prior spoken text (one's own or the other speaker's) projects and shapes subsequent talk.

It is hoped that this collection will be a springboard for more thinking about ways to untangle gender and context and to show their interconnectedness as well. For example, one approach would be to study the discourse of individual speakers in different natural situations with different partners, for example, comparing someone talking with friends and with siblings. This would surely help us to understand how gendered speech might be adaptive to the particularities of the discourse context.

GENDER

The articles in this issue focus attention on what are actually deceptively simple and elusive ideas about gender. Implicit in this collection is an unexamined working assumption that there is a fairly coherent set of implicit beliefs, stereotypes, prohibitions or prescriptions that adults in a speech community understand, or can agree on, that define what "gender" means — or perhaps should mean — in that community. It is not clear how accurate this assumption is or how trouble-free the concept of gender is. Furthermore, gender prescriptions surely are oversimplifications, as are all stereotypes. Human beings are far more complicated and adaptive in actual social interaction. To complicate things further, our ideas of gender-appropriateness can and do change over our lifetime. Thus, researchers need to more closely examine: (1) what we mean by gender, and (2) how we conceptualize the "match" between (a) superficial and general social prescriptions for conventionally "appropriate" gendered behavior and (b) the complex interactional choices human beings make in specific situations that might reflect, resist, or even ignore conventional social prescriptions about gender.

For all of the exciting questions that this collection of articles raises, it nevertheless makes clear that peer talk and parent–child talk are key contexts that create shared knowledge about gender norms, teaching young children to act in mutually acceptable ways and giving opportunities for self-expression that is shaped by those norms.

CONCLUSION

Thinking about gender is complicated. Studying talk is not easy either. The analysis of everyday conversational contexts shows how ordinary conversations provide occasions for young children to learn about and to "do" being a girl or boy. In exploring how discourse is a medium of socialization, this collection also brings us back to our own sociolinguistic roots.

REFERENCES

Fishman, P. M. (1983). Interaction: The work women do. In B. Thorne, C. Kramarae, & N. Henley (Eds.), *Language, gender and society* (pp. 89–101). Rowley, MA: Newbury House.

Goodwin, M. H. (1980). Directive-response speech sequences in girls' and boys' task activities. In S. McConnell-Ginet, R. Borker, & N. Furman (Eds.), *Women and language in literature and society* (pp. 157–174). New York: Praeger.

Thorne, B. (1986). Girls and boys together . . . but mostly apart: Gender arrangements in elementary schools. In W. Hartup & Z. Rubin (Eds.), *Relationships and development* (pp. 167–184). Hillsdale, NJ: Lawrence Erlbaum Associates, Inc.

Sheldon, A. (1990). Pickle fights: Gendered talk in preschool disputes. *Discourse Processes, 13,* 5–31.

Sheldon, A. (1992). Conflict talk: Sociolinguistic challenges to self-assertion and how young girls meet them. *Merrill-Palmer Quarterly, 38,* 95–117.

Research on Language and Social Interaction, 29(1), 7–25
Copyright © 1996, Lawrence Erlbaum Associates, Inc.

"Why Didn't You Talk to Your Mommy, Honey?": Parents' and Children's Talk About Talk

Richard Ely
Department of Psychology
Boston University

Jean Berko Gleason
Department of Psychology
Boston University

Allyssa McCabe
Department of Psychology
University of Massachusetts–Lowell and Harvard University

In this article, we focus on a characteristic of narrative style that is associated with gender. In a number of studies of White working-class and middle-class children and adults, we have found that females use far more reported speech or dialogue than males do in their personal narratives (Ely & McCabe, 1993; Ely, Gleason, Narasimhan, & McCabe, 1995). In telling stories about past events, girls and women commonly include what someone said. Narratives are an important way of conveying one's interpretation of the world, particularly the world of the past, and variations in narrative style that are characteristic of a

Correspondence concerning this article should be sent to Richard Ely, Department of Psychology, Boston University, 64 Cummington Street, Boston, MA 02215. E-mail: rely@asc.bu.edu group or culture may reflect differences in how members view themselves, their communities, and their past (Michaels, 1981; McCabe, 1991, 1996). The goal of this article is to describe this gendered difference in storytelling and to explore the possible reasons for its occurrence, focusing in particular on parent–child interaction in a longitudinal study of 10 families.

Although this study provides some sense of how gender differences are transmitted from parent to child, we move beyond these empirical findings to speculate about possible explanations for the origins and functions of these differences. In doing this, we draw on some of our earlier studies of language socialization, including work on parents' use of prohibitives and diminutives in speech to girls and boys. In the earlier work, we found, for instance, that when trying to prevent their young child from doing something, mothers are more likely to say "NO!" or "Stop that!" to little boys, but to be much gentler with little girls (Gleason, Ely, Perlmann, & Narasimhan, in press). We also found when we examined diminutives (words like *footie* and *doggie*) in parents' speech to little girls and boys, that the parents used more of these affectionate terms with little girls (Gleason, Perlmann, Ely, & Evans, 1994). The differential use of prohibitives, diminutives, and references to certain kinds of events in the past, such as conversations, constitutes a subtle kind of socialization. This enculturation may occur pervasively as children acquire their roles as females and males. Speech to young children shapes their world view and provides them with models of how women and men talk (Gleason, 1988; Ely & Gleason, 1995).

REPORTED SPEECH

In reported speech, a speaker makes explicit reference to a past speech event. Reported speech is essentially talk about past talk and can take several forms. In *direct speech,* the speaker typically "demonstrates" what someone did in saying something (Clark & Gerrig, 1990). Direct speech is usually enclosed within quotation marks in written discourse.

> . . . and then Dad come in 'cause Grant was crying and **he said, "[Get] in your own beds."**[1]

Indirect speech allows greater latitude in the match between the quotation and the original utterance. Indirect speech is often marked linguistically by the use of a nominal or infinitive clause, or by transpositions in syntactic person or verb tense.

> . . . and once I put it [gum] under my pillow and then I ate, ate some and **he told me to give him the package** . . .

In using indirect speech, narrators can suggest their interpretation of past speech by quoting selectively from the original utterance (Vološinov, 1986). Even in direct speech, a speaker can quote an utterance word for word but give different emphases to particular elements, by, for instance, stressing particular words (Clark & Gerrig, 1990).

In addition to using direct and indirect speech, it is also possible to refer to past speech by simply indicating that it took place. This form of reported speech is termed *narratized speech* (Genette, 1988). Although narratized speech often masks the sense or feel of the original utterance, the use of particular speech verbs can convey particular impressions.

> Mother: **What did you call** your cousin Carolyn when you were up there?

Here the mother's choice of speech verb implicates a characterization of a past speech event as having including name-calling. Thus, through a variety of forms, utterances from the past can be rephrased in new contexts, often with reinterpreted meanings and intents (Tannen, 1989).

It is important to note that both empirical evidence and theoretical accounts argue against the notion that *any* form of reported speech is based on a totally accurate recollection of past speech, or on the actual occurrence of a past speech event (Sachs, 1967; Neisser, 1981; Tannen, 1989; Clark & Gerrig, 1990). Memory for the surface structure of ordinary speech has been shown to be poor in experimental settings (Sachs, 1967) and in extended conversational discourse (Neisser, 1981), although the semantic content is often well preserved. However, the exact wording of nonroutine, humorous, and highly personal remarks may be more readily retained (Keenan, MacWhinney, & Mayhew, 1977). Tannen (1989, p. 110) contended that reported speech is best considered "constructed dialogue." Clark and Gerrig (1990) held that quotations are "selective depictions" that are not necessarily designed to reproduce a particular utterance accurately. Therefore, all forms of reported speech could be regarded as a part of the sense-making nature of memories (Bartlett, 1932; Neisser, 1982; Bruner, 1986). Conversational reports of past speech thus encompass verbatim quotations, loose interpretations or summations of what was once said (often in the form of indirect speech), as well as creative constructions of what might have been, could have been, or should have been said.

GENDER DIFFERENCES IN REPORTED SPEECH

Data on gender differences in memory for past speech are sparse. Examination of the psychology literature reveals few relevant findings. Although there is some evidence that women *believe* they are better at remembering conversations than men (Crawford, Herrimann, Holdsworth, Randall, & Robbins, 1989), experimental data do not support this belief (Goldsmith & Pillemer, 1988). Even though women may be no more accurate than men in remembering the wording of conversations, they are more likely to refer to them in their personal narratives. For example, Goodwin's (1990) study of verbal disputes among African-American inner-city children found that girls were the primary participants in "he-said-she-said" confrontations. Similarly, in a study of the narratives of middle-class White Americans, Johnstone (1993) found that women included reports of speech more frequently than men did. By including (and in some instances creating) what was once said, women and men portray different worlds. "People in women's stories have names, and they sit around and talk; people in men's stories are more often nameless, and their environment is more silent" (Johnstone, 1993, p. 73). These findings in the literature suggest that in working- and middle-class communities the inclination to use reported speech varies according to the gender of the speaker.

In our own recent work, we also have found pronounced gender differences in the citation of past speech. In a study of the narratives of working-class children from rural Ohio, we found that girls used reported speech at twice the rate of boys (Ely & McCabe, 1993). They quoted themselves, their mothers, and other children more than boys did. In using reported speech, girls were more likely to use direct speech and less likely to use indirect speech.

In this same study, we found an intriguing pattern in children's quotation of parents' speech. In the narratives of both boys and girls, there was a proportional drop with age in quotations of the mothers' speech, a drop that was concurrent with (but not necessarily an artifact of) a rise in quotations of fathers' speech. In other words, the younger children were more likely to quote their mothers than their fathers, and this was especially true of girls. We interpret this pattern as further evidence that mothers speak to toddlers more than fathers do and that they speak to their daughters more than they do to their sons (Fagot & Hagan, 1991). Quotations of fathers increased with age in girls' narratives. However, in boys' narratives, quotations of their fathers' speech were minimally present at all ages. The relatively low rate of reports of father's speech by both girls and boys is consistent with research that documents fathers' low rate of interaction with their young children (Ninio & Rinott, 1988).

In another study, we examined reported speech in the dinnertime conversations of 22 White middle-class families with at least one preschool child (Ely et al., 1995). Again, there were dramatic gender differences in the frequency of reported speech. Mothers reported memories of past speech at twice the rate of fathers and four times the rate of children. Among children (whose overall rate of quotation was not high), girls quoted past speech at twice the rate of boys, although this difference was not statistically different because of the small numbers involved. In looking at differences in proportional frequencies in how mothers, fathers, and children quoted past speech, we found that mothers were more likely to use indirect speech and fathers were more inclined merely to note that a past speech event had occurred.

In addition to using higher rates of quotations, mothers' (but not fathers') use of reported speech at dinner was positively correlated with their children's use of reported speech in those same conversations. Examination of the data indicated that this correlation was due in great part to children's high rate of compliance with mothers' prompts and queries. Although this finding should be viewed tentatively, given the small number of children who quoted past speech, it nevertheless is consonant with recent research that documents how parents influence their children's narratives across a variety of domains (Snow & Dickinson, 1990; Fivush, 1991; McCabe & Peterson, 1991; Peterson & McCabe, 1992).

In the study we present here, we draw on these findings. We hypothesized that parents' attention to reported speech in their elicitation of narratives from their young children would be positively associated with children's use of quotations in narratives elicited by an interviewer. If there is a relationship between parents' use of references to past talk and children's subsequent use of such references with an experimenter, we have support for the hypothesis that parents' verbal style affects their children's style. In addition to testing this association, we also sought to derive information about the form and function of quotations in children's experimenter-elicited narratives.

METHODS

Subjects and Procedure

The 10 subjects (5 girls, 5 boys) were from middle-class Canadian families with children who are part of an ongoing longitudinal study of children's narratives (Peterson & McCabe, 1992). The children were between the ages of 2;1 and 2;3 at the outset of data collection. For the first 18 months of this study, parents were provided tape recorders and blank tapes and asked to record narratives about past events as naturally as possible on a monthly basis. These conversations took place in the families' home and were generally initiated by the parents (e.g., "Cara, when we went to the hospital last week, what did you see there?"). In addition to these data, all families were visited at regular intervals by an experimenter, who sought to elicit narratives during an hour-long play session. In the course of routine conversation, the experimenter inserted prompts that have been found in past research to generate stories about the past (e.g., "Have you ever fallen and hurt yourself? You have? Tell me about it . . ."; Peterson & McCabe, 1983, 1992). The experimenter did not scaffold the children's narratives and provided only limited feedback indicative of general interest and encouragement (e.g., "Uh-huh . . . and? . . . And then what happened?").

Data

Data analyzed included all the discourse associated with parent-elicited narratives when the children were between the ages of 2;1 and

3;7, as well as the narratives elicited by the experimenter when the children were 3;0, 3;7, and 5;0. A parent-elicited narrative was defined as a "discussion about a different experience (i.e., one taking place at a different time and place)" (Peterson & McCabe, 1992, p. 305) and included all the parents' and children's utterances included in the "discussions." For the interviewer-elicited narratives, a narrative was defined as two or more utterances recounting a specific past event (Labov & Waletzky, 1967; Peterson & McCabe, 1983, 1992).

Coding

Reported speech was defined as any linguistically marked re-counting of a past speech event. This generally requires use of a speech verb (e.g., *to say, to tell, to ask*), but could also be achieved through contextual and syntactic cues and/or changes in person or tense (e.g., "[He] said: 'Spell you(r) name'. [I said]: 'N-I-C-K-Y'.").

Reported speech that used the historical present tense (e.g., "And I scr(eamed) . . . and I [hit her] and say: 'Brada don't you dare do that again, Brada'.") and was embedded within narratives was included. Reports in response to a question about a specific speech event in the past were also included.

> Mother: Did you see her? And what did you say to Kiah?
> Cara: Happy Birthday.

Parental Prompts

Parental prompts focusing on past speech events were coded as *speech-related* or *general*. Speech-related prompts were further coded as either open- or closed-ended (Dickinson, 1991).

An *open-ended* prompt identifies instances where the parent asks the child about the content of a speech event, seeking to elicit a report of past speech:

> What else did you do with Pam? What did you talk about?

In contrast, a *closed-ended* prompt merely asks if a speech event took place or asks for clarification or confirmation about a past speech event:

Did you talk to Nonnie on the phone this morning?

A child's quotation of a past speech event that was the initial response to a general (not speech-related) prompt was noted as such:

Mother: Why didn't you want her to do that [to wash the dishes]?
Kelly: Cause I told her to find something else [to do].

Finally, reports of past speech unrelated to parental prompts or embedded in multiple utterances following a parental prompt were coded as *spontaneous*.

Other Coding

In addition to the coding of parental prompts in parent-elicited narratives, we also coded each instance of reported speech in the children's experimenter-elicited narratives for form (direct, indirect, and narratized), type of reported speech act (e.g., assertive, directive) and use of speech verb, as well as the identity of the reported speaker. A more detailed description of coding categories and procedures can be found in Ely and McCabe (1993).

Reliability

Interrater reliability was conducted on a sample of more than one-third of the data. Cohen's kappas for the coding of the form of reported speech, the reported speech act, and the category of parental prompt were .89, .82, and .81, respectively, representing "almost perfect" interrater agreement (Landis & Koch, 1977, p. 165).

RESULTS

Parent-Elicited Narratives

There were 566 parent-elicited narratives ($M = 57$, $SD = 38$) produced by all children over the 18-month period. Recall that in the parent-initiated conversations about the past, narratives were defined as discussions about a particular past event, and the data analyzed included all parental utterances (prompts and comments) about the particular events. Although both parents were urged to participate, the majority of the narratives were elicited by mothers (see Table 1). In addition, there was wide variation in the rate of parents' submissions of tapes to the research team (Table 1).

In the parent-initiated discussions about past events, parents produced 107 prompts ($M = 10.7$, $SD = 11.0$) about past speech events (Table 2). Most of these prompts (100) were made by mothers. In addition, parents themselves made 55 reports of past speech ($M = 5.5$, $SD = 5.8$) in talking about the past with their children. Again, the majority of these reports (50) were made by mothers. Taken together, prompts about past speech events and the spontaneous use of reported speech represent parents' attention to past speech.

Experimenter-Elicited Narratives

Children produced an overall total of 364 narratives ($M = 36$, $SD = 9$) with the interviewer at ages 3;0, 3;7, and 5;0. In these narratives, there were 70 reports of past speech or a mean of 7.0 ($SD = 6.2$) per child. Only three children (two boys, one girl) did not report past speech

TABLE 1
Parent-Elicited Narratives: Study 3

Subject	Number of Tapes Submitted	Age Range (Months)	Number of Narratives Elicited by		
			Mother	Father	Mixed[a]
Girls					
Cara	12	28–43	89	38	8
Kelly	9	28–44	49	4	0
Sally	2	25–31	9	5	0
Harriet	11	26–38	82	2	0
Leah	7	26–42	82	2	0
Boys					
Ned	11	26–38	48	0	0
Paul	11	30–43	32	7	35
Gary	7	28–43	19	1	0
Terry	5	27–39	6	12	0
Carl	10	26–42	34	2	0

[a]Both parents participating together.

TABLE 2
Parents' Attention to Past Speech and Children's Use of Reported Speech in
Interviewer-Elicited Narratives: Study 3

	Parents' Attention to Past Speech		Children's Reported Speech in Experimenter-Elicited Narratives
	Prompts	Reported Speech	
Girls			
Cara	11	16	15
Kelly	22	3	6
Sally	0	0	0
Harriet	33	4	6
Leah	4	14	13
Boys			
Ned	20	5	16
Paul	9	10	4
Gary	1	0	0
Terry	0	2	0
Carl	7	1	10

(see Table 2). Of the 70 reports of past speech, 46 (65.7%) occurred in the narratives told at age 5;0, 18 (25.7%) were produced at age 3;7, and only 6 (8.6%) were produced in the narratives told at age 3;0.

Correlations

Simple correlations were run to test the association between parents' attention to past speech events and children's independent use of reported speech in unscaffolded narratives with an experimenter. Both raw and proportional frequencies were used in the correlational analyses. Raw frequencies capture the extent to which parents talked with their children about the past in general and reported speech in particular (as reflected in the number of tapes and the narratives contained therein that were submitted to the research team) (Hoff-Ginsberg, 1992). During the interviews with the experimenter, each child had an equal number of opportunities to produce narratives in general as well as reported speech in particular. In contrast to raw frequencies, proportional frequencies (rates of reported speech or parental prompts per narrative) standardize the individual variation in the amount of data obtained and analyzed. Thus, each measure describes a different aspect of the same phenomenon (Pine, 1992).

Using raw frequencies, there was a positive correlation in the predicted direction, $r(10) = .60, p < .07$, between parental attention to past speech in conversations with their children (ages 2;1 to 3;7) and children's unprompted use of reported speech with an interviewer at ages 3;0, 3;7, and 5;0. A correlation using proportional frequencies (number of prompts or reports per narrative) generated similar results, $r(10) = .57, p < .09$. Because the majority (65.7%) of occurrences of reported speech were found in the narratives told when the children were age 5;0, a simple correlation was run between parental attention to past speech and the 46 reports of past speech in children's experimenter-elicited narratives at age 5;0. As hypothesized, there was a positive relationship between the two variables, $r(10) = .68, p < .04$ (raw frequencies). A correlational analysis using proportional frequencies was in the predicted direction but did not reach statistical significance, $r(10) = .35, p = .32$. Taken together, these analyses indicate that the children whose parents frequently asked questions about past conversations or used reported speech were generally the same children who later were likely to talk spontaneously about past speech events in their experimenter-elicited narratives.

Descriptive data regarding the form, identity of reported speaker, reported speech act, and speech verbs in the experimenter-elicited narratives are presented in Table 3. In general, the data support findings in our earlier studies (Ely & McCabe, 1993; Ely et al., 1995). For example, children quoted themselves and other children more frequently than any other category of speaker, a pattern that is similar to that found in quotations in children's dinnertime conversations (Ely et al., 1995). In form, direct speech was the most frequently used type of quotation, again in line with findings from earlier studies of preschool and school-aged children (Ely & McCabe, 1993; Ely et al., 1995). One notable difference between figures in the current study and figures from earlier work is the high rate of reported speech from imaginary characters. This was a result of the interview protocol itself, which called for the experimenter to elicit a made-up or fantasy narrative.

Gender Differences

Because the bulk of what has been termed *parents'* attention represents *mothers'* attention, the correlational finding reported here primarily represents associations between mothers' and children's speech behaviors. There were other noteworthy gender differences. For exam-

TABLE 3
Frequencies of Categories of Children's Reported Speech in
Experimenter-Elicited Narratives: Study 3

Identity of speaker	
Self	18 (25.7)[a]
Mother	6 (8.6)
Father	5 (7.1)
Other children	19 (27.1)
Other adults	8 (11.4)
Pet, imaginary figure	14 (20.0)
Form	
Direct	40 (57.1)
Indirect	17 (24.3)
Narratized	13 (18.6)
Speech act	
Assertive	25 (35.7)
Directive	23 (32.9)
Commissive	2 (2.9)
Expressive	5 (7.1)
Declaration	3 (4.3)
Summarized	12 (17.1)
Speech verb	
to say	50 (71.4)
to tell	10 (14.3)
All others[b]	10 (14.3)

[a]Figures in parentheses are percentage of column totals.
[b]Only 1 of 70 occurrences of reported speech was unmarked.

ple, parental prompts to girls ($M = 14$, $SD = 13.5$) were nearly twice as frequent as prompts to boys ($M = 7.4$, $SD = 8.0$). Not surprisingly, girls' prompted reports of past speech ($M = 7.6$, $SD = 5.9$) occurred at a rate double that of boys ($M = 3.2$, $SD = 4.7$). With the experimenter, girls ($M = 8.0$, $SD = 6.0$) used reported speech at a rate only slightly higher than that of boys ($M = 6.0$, $SD = 6.9$). A closer examination of the data revealed that boys' quotations were far more common at ages 3;0 and 3;7. By age 5;0, the rate of girls' use of reported speech was more than double that of boys, $M_{girls} = 6.6$ ($SD = 5.3$) versus $M_{boys} = 2.6$ ($SD = 5.8$). Given the small number of subjects, these gender differences were not statistically significant and should be viewed with caution. However, it is of interest to note that in this small sample, although younger children report speech at similar rates, by the time they are 5, girls' attention to speech, as reflected in their use of reported speech, is double that of boys.

DISCUSSION

This article has shown one of the subtle ways in which language addressed to boys and girls differ: Girls' attention is turned to speech, to what they and others have said. These are not the only differences in the socialization of boys and girls that we have seen in studies of parents and children. For example, parents use more inner-state, emotional words with girls than with boys (Dunn, Bretherton, & Munn, 1987; Schell & Gleason, 1989), direct more diminutives and terms of endearment to girls than to boys (Warren-Leubecker, 1982; Gleason et al., 1994), and use weaker and less frequent prohibitions to girls than to boys (Gleason et al., in press). Through interactions such as these, parents express and perpetuate specific cultural and gender-based standards. Such standards are not typically recognizable to either participants or researchers in any single observation, but become apparent only over time and only when the particular behaviors (e.g., talking about emotions, prohibiting, using diminutives, talking about talking) are noted to vary according to the child's gender. One way to account for these differences in parental speech is to posit that the parents of boys and the parents of girls make different assumptions about their children. For instance parents may believe that their daughters are sensitive, emotional, and interested in others, and that their sons are comparatively tough and uninterested in inner feelings and other people. Whether these parental beliefs are a reflection of some actual innate differences between the sexes or are a purely social construct is beyond the scope of this article. As the earlier research showed, daughters hear more diminutives and are called by more loving pet names. Boys hear more imperatives and are often addressed in a less kind and gentle fashion. Here we have shown that girls are more likely to be directed to what they and others have said. It is, of course, a given in our society that "girls are more verbal than boys," even though empirical research on early language has shown few differences (Hyde & Linn, 1988).

Children may come with different predispositions, but parents can choose to amplify or to mitigate any inborn differences that exist. In the case of gender differences in language, parents may be amplifying — or perhaps even creating — differences through differential socialization. In addition, it is important to recognize that parents are not the only socializing forces in children's lives. For example, in this study, parents may have been responding to gender-specific traits that their children acquired from interactions with peers and the media.

When we looked at references to speech itself, we found that parents who asked questions about past conversations and who reported past speech in talking with their children had children who were likely to include dialogue in the personal narratives they told to an experimenter. In some instances, parents' attention to past speech was in the form of a series of persistent prompts followed by parent-provided responses or comments, as seen in Carl's mother's efforts when he was 2;6:

> Mother: Can you tell me what you and Paula talked about? Did you tell Paula about going to Bowering Park? Cause she said you didn't tell her. That would have been something nice to tell her.

Another mother delivered a similar flurry of questions to her daughter, also aged 2;6:

> Mother: Did the walk make you tired yesterday? What did you say to me all the way home in the car yesterday? Do you remember? Do you remember what you said to me? I'm what?
> Harriet: Go in the car.
> Mother: Yes when you were in the car what did you say though? Did you say, "I'm tired"? Hey? Did you say, "I'm tired"? Is that what you said? Why were you tired Harriet?

In a third example, a mother reprimanded her 29-month-old daughter for having scratched another child:

> Mother: Why were we upset?
> Cara: At me ((pause)) ask Anthony.
> Mother: We wanted you to ask Anthony. We wanted you to talk to him, [to] tell him what the problem was.
> Cara: I wasn't mad.

In these examples, the child's own speech (or lack of speech in Cara's case) was the focus of parents' attention. In the first example, Carl's mother gently admonished him for not having said something that "would have been nice to tell." In the second example, Harriet's mother tried to get Harriet to acknowledge that she had said that she was tired the day before. In the third example, Cara's mother talked about the importance of "using your words." All mothers appear to be using past speech as a vehicle for socialization, in the first instance to inform the child about the importance of making *nice* conversation, in the second instance to instill a deeper understanding of the importance of not becoming overtired, and in the third instance, to emphasize the value of talking about feelings.

In narratives elicited by an experimenter two and one-half years later, these same three children all used reported speech. For example, Carl reported how someone "guessed" what he had been for Halloween:

Carl: Um, I, do you know what, do you know he said?
Experimenter: What did he say?
Carl: What am I and he guessed right. A teenage ninja
                turtle Raphael.

In telling a story about a dog, Harriet said: "My sister just says, 'Look, I think that's a German shepherd'." Cara told a story about staying up late that included several references to a young child's speech: "And when I came back Ian said, 'Hug' . . . and I don't know what he is saying . . . because he mostly speaks baby talk."

This relation between parents' talk about talk and children's later use of quotations in their narratives extends the range of specific features of children's narratives that have been shown to be associated with parental input. A more intriguing (and more speculative) finding is the possible evidence for how a gender-specific pattern of narrative may be passed from parents (primarily mothers) to their children. Mothers more than fathers talk about past speech in conversing about the past with their children, and parents (mothers and fathers) prompt girls about past speech more than they do boys. Although the rates of quotations in girls' and boys' speech are approximately similar at age three in this small sample, by age five, girls are quoting past speech at twice the rate of boys.

Past speech is a tangible, reportable event, as worthy of attention as any other past action or event. Our research has shown that in a variety of contexts, working- and middle-class North American females place greater emphasis on reporting speech events than do males. It is possible that this difference is due solely to women's greater propensity to talk about the past (Ross & Holmberg, 1990), although this cannot account for the robust gender differences we found in our analyses of an extensive corpus of narratives from children (Ely & McCabe, 1993). In those analyses, girls reported speech at more than twice the rate of boys on a standardized measure of narrative length. We believe that in the communities we have studied, the greater attention women and girls appear to pay to speech is likely to be a product of differential socialization. Mothers were the primary caretakers of children in the families we studied here and were the primary caretakers in the working- and middle-class households studied earlier. There is evidence that mothers, more than fathers, encourage and support communication with their young children, especially their daughters (Fagot & Hagan, 1991), a phenomenon that we found echoed in our finding that parents (mostly mothers) prompted their girls about past speech twice as frequently as boys.

Furthermore, in this article, we have found preliminary evidence that this gender difference is reinstated through the telling and retelling of stories about the past, particularly in the stories that are shared between mothers and their children (Turner, 1981; McCabe & Peterson, 1991). Some (Shils, 1981) have argued that communities are sustained through "resayings." If resayings are essential to society and its understanding of itself and its past, then women and girls appear to be carrying a larger part of the responsibility for this task. In talking about the past, they fill their stories with people with voices. In contrast, men appear more willing to fill their stories with people with muted voices. Thus, when women experience silence, they wonder and ask, as Kelly's mother did: "Why didn't you talk to your Mommy, Honey?"

NOTE

1   All examples come from the data.

REFERENCES

Bartlett, F. C. (1932). *Remembering*. Cambridge: Cambridge University Press.
Bruner, J. (1986). *Actual minds, possible worlds*. Cambridge, MA: Harvard University Press.

Clark, H. H., & Gerrig, R. J. (1990). Quotations as demonstrations. *Language, 66,* 764–805.

Crawford, M., Herrimann, D. J., Holdsworth, M. J., Randall, E. P., & Robbins, D. (1989). Gender and beliefs about memory. *British Journal of Psychology, 80,* 391–401.

Dickinson, D. K. (1991). Teacher agenda and setting: Constraints on conversation in preschools. In A. McCabe & C. Peterson (Eds.), *Developing narrative structure* (pp. 255–302). Hillsdale, NJ: Lawrence Erlbaum Associates, Inc.

Dunn, J., Bretherton, I., & Munn, P. (1987). Conversations about feeling states between mothers and their young children. *Developmental Psychology, 23,* 132–139.

Ely, R., & Gleason, J. B. (1995). Socialization across contexts. In P. Fletcher & B. MacWhinney (Eds.), *Handbook of child language* (pp. 251–270). Oxford: Blackwell.

Ely, R., Gleason, J. B., Narasimhan, B., & McCabe, A. (1995). Family talk about talk: Mothers lead the way. *Discourse Processes, 19,* 201–218.

Ely, R., & McCabe, A. (1993). Remembered voices. *Journal of Child Language, 20,* 671–696.

Fagot, B. I., & Hagan, R. (1991). Observations of parent reactions to sex-stereotyped behaviors: Age and sex effects. *Child Development, 62,* 617–628.

Fivush, R. (1991). The social construction of personal narratives. *Merrill-Palmer Quarterly, 37,* 59–81.

Genette, G. (1988). *Narrative discourse revisited.* Ithaca, NY: Cornell University Press.

Gleason, J. B. (1988). Language and socialization. In F. S. Kessel (Ed.), *The development of language and language researchers: Essays in honor of Roger Brown* (pp. 269–280). Hillsdale, NJ: Lawrence Erlbaum Associates, Inc.

Gleason, J. B., Ely, R., Perlmann, R. Y., & Narasimhan, B. (in press). Patterns of prohibitions in parent–child discourse. In D. I. Slobin, J. Gerhardt, A. Kyratzis, & J. Guo (Eds.), *Social interaction, social context, and language: Essays in honor of Susan Ervin-Tripp.* Mahwah, NJ: Lawrence Erlbaum Associates, Inc.

Gleason, J. B., Perlmann, R. Y., Ely, R., & Evans, D. W. (1994). The babytalk register: Parents' use of diminutives. In J. Sokolov & C. Snow (Eds.), *Handbook of research in language using CHILDES* (pp. 50–76). Hillsdale, NJ: Lawrence Erlbaum Associates, Inc.

Goldsmith, L. R., & Pillemer, D. B. (1988). Memories of statements spoken in everyday contexts. *Applied Cognitive Psychology, 2,* 273–286.

Goodwin, M. H. (1990). *He-said-she-said: Talk as social organization among Black children.* Bloomington: Indiana University Press.

Hoff-Ginsberg, E. (1992). How should input frequency be measured? *First Language, 12,* 233–244.

Hyde, J. S., & Linn, M. C. (1988). Gender differences in verbal ability: A meta-analysis. *Psychological Bulletin, 104,* 53–69.

Johnstone, B. (1993). Community and contest: Midwestern men and women creating their worlds in conversational storytelling. In D. Tannen (Ed.), *Gender and conversational interaction* (pp. 62–80). New York: Oxford University Press.

Keenan, J. M., MacWhinney, B., & Mayhew, D. (1977). Pragmatics in memory: A study of natural conversation. *Journal of Verbal Learning and Verbal Behavior, 16,* 549–560.

Labov, W., & Waletzky, J. (1967). Narrative analysis. In J. Helm (Ed.), *Essays on the verbal and visual arts* (pp. 12–44). Seattle: University of Washington Press.

Landis, J. R., & Koch, G. G. (1977). The measurement of observer agreement for categorical data. *Biometrics, 33,* 159–174.

McCabe, A. (1991). Preface: Structure as a way of understanding. In A. McCabe & C. Peterson (Eds.), *Developing narrative structure* (pp. ix–xvii). Hillsdale, NJ: Lawrence Erlbaum Associates, Inc.

McCabe, A. (1996). *Chameleon readers: Teaching children to appreciate all kinds of good stories.* New York: McGraw-Hill.

McCabe, A., & Peterson, C. (1991). Getting the story: A longitudinal study of parental styles in eliciting narratives and developing narrative skill. In A. McCabe & C. Peterson (Eds.), *Developing narrative structure* (pp. 217–253). Hillsdale, NJ: Lawrence Erlbaum Associates, Inc.

Michaels, S. (1981). "Sharing Time": Children's narrative styles and differential access to literacy. *Language in Society, 10,* 423–442.

Neisser, U. (1981). John Dean's memory: A case study. *Cognition, 9,* 1–22.

Neisser, U. (1982). Memory: What are the important questions? In U. Neisser (Ed.), *Memory observed: Remembering in natural contexts* (pp. 3–19). New York: W. H. Freeman.

Ninio, A., & Rinott, N. (1988). Fathers' involvement in the care of their infants and their attributions of cognitive competence. *Child Development, 59,* 652–663.

Peterson, C., & McCabe, A. (1983). *Developmental psycholinguistics: Three ways of looking at a child's narrative.* New York: Plenum.

Peterson, C., & McCabe, A. (1992). Parental styles of narrative elicitation: Effect on children's narrative structure and content. *First Language, 12,* 299–321.

Pine, J. M. (1992). Commentary on: How should input frequency be measured? *First Language, 12,* 245–249.

Ross, M., & Holmberg, D. (1990). Recounting the past: Gender differences in the recall of events in the history of a close relationship. In M. P. Zanna & J. M. Olson (Eds.), *The Ontario Symposium: Vol. 6. Self-inferences processes* (pp. 135–152). Hillsdale, NJ: Lawrence Erlbaum Associates, Inc.

Sachs, J. (1967). Recognition memory for syntactic and semantic aspects of connective discourse. *Perception and Psychophysics, 2,* 437–442.

Schell, A., & Gleason, J. B. (1989, January). *Gender differences in the acquisition of the vocabulary of emotion.* Paper presented at the annual meeting of the American Association of Applied Linguistics, Washington, DC.

Shils, E. A. (1981). *Tradition*. Chicago: University of Chicago Press.

Snow, C. E., & Dickinson, D. K. (1990). Literacy and language: Relationships during the preschool years. *Harvard Educational Review, 53,* 165–189.

Tannen, D. (1989). *Talking voices: Repetition, dialogue and imagery in conversational discourse*. Cambridge, England: Cambridge University Press.

Turner, V. (1981). Social dramas and stories about them. In W. J. T. Mitchell (Ed.), *On narrative* (pp. 137–164). Chicago: University of Chicago Press.

Vološinov, V. N. (1986). *Marxism and the philosophy of language*. Cambridge, MA: Harvard University Press.

Warren-Leubecker, A. (1982). *Sex differences in speech to children*. Unpublished master's thesis, Georgia Institute of Technology, Atlanta.

Research on Language and Social Interaction, 29(1), 27–56

Mothers, Fathers, Daughters, Sons: Gender Differences in Autobiographical Reminiscing

Elaine Reese
Department of Psychology
University of Otago

Catherine A. Haden and Robyn Fivush
Department of Psychology
Emory University

As adults, we tell stories about past happenings in our lives for a variety of reasons: to entertain others with our triumphs and disappointments, to inform others of our version of events when the facts are in dispute, and to recreate with others the emotional bonds of a shared history. Recounting past events is primarily a shared activity and serves important social functions (see also Pillemer & White, 1989; Middleton & Edwards, 1990; Nelson, 1993; Fivush, Haden, & Reese, in press).

This research was funded by a grant from the Spencer Foundation to Robyn Fivush. Many people were involved in various aspects of this study, but we especially thank Liza Dondonan for her help in data collection, Marcella Eppen and Laura Underwood for their help in transcription, and Janet Kuebli for her conceptual input. We are also grateful to all the families who generously gave of their time throughout this project.

Correspondence concerning this article should be sent to Elaine Reese, Department of Psychology, University of Otago, New Zealand. E-mail to Ereese@rivendeli.otago.ac.nz

Importantly, men and women exhibit qualitative and quantitative differences in their reported autobiographical memories. When asked to recall memories from early childhood, women recall a greater number of such memories and date those memories back to an earlier age than do men (Cowan & Davidson, 1984; Friedman & Pines, 1991; Mullen, 1994). Women's stories of the past may also be richer than men's. Friedman and Pines found that women wrote longer accounts of their early memories than did men, and Ross and Holmberg (1990), in a study of married couples, showed that women's descriptions of shared memories were judged by independent raters to be more accurate and more vivid than men's accounts. Together, these findings suggest that women produce longer and more detailed accounts of past events, whether shared or unshared, from childhood or from adulthood, when asked to reflect on such experiences than do men.

Ross and Holmberg (1990) concluded that these gender differences in reminiscing may reflect a greater value that women place on the activity of talking about the past. These results seem related to recent claims by Tannen (1990) and Gilligan (1982), among others, that men and women have a different "voice" in a number of arenas, including different conversational styles and moral reasoning styles. Specifically, women may have a more affiliative than instrumental style of conversing and reasoning than men, although these gender differences vary depending on context and task (e.g., Galotti, Kozberg, & Farmer, 1991; Johnson, 1994). An intriguing possibility, then, is that gender differences in reminiscing stem from the inherently linguistic and communicative nature of the activity. Even if men and women have similar experiences, they may choose to talk about different aspects of those experiences in greater detail, or structure their stories of the past in different ways.

Given that these differences in reminiscing occur even for memories from early childhood, at what point in development does this difference between females and males arise, and how might it come about? One possibility is that parents socialize girls and boys into different styles of reminiscing. Parents and children begin talking about the past very early in development (e.g., Sachs, 1983; Hudson, 1990) and these discussions are pervasive in early parent–child interactions in a number of cultures (Eisenberg, 1985; Engel, 1986; Miller & Sperry, 1988; Miller, Potts, Fung, Hoogstra, & Mintz, 1990). The study of mothers' and fathers' conversations about the past with sons and daughters across the preschool period may thus help illuminate various aspects of gender differences in reminiscing.

First, in light of the research demonstrating gender differences in adults, we can assess whether mothers and fathers differ in their styles of talking about the past. Do men and women retain their differences in reminiscing when speaking about the past with their young children? Second, we can address questions regarding the early socialization of memories and investigate parents' different styles of conversing with their daughters and sons. Are parents socializing daughters to reminisce about past events in a richer manner than sons? Finally, we can examine evidence for possible early gender differences in reminiscing by contrasting girls' and boys' remembering; girls and boys may differ in the amount of information they recall.

Only one study to date has examined mothers' and fathers' styles of talking about the past with daughters and sons. Reese and Fivush (1993) found that parents displayed a great deal of variability in the degree to which they elaborated on past events with their children aged 3;4. The following excerpts from those conversations help illustrate the overall tone of these highly elaborative and less elaborative parental styles of conversing about the past. The first two examples illustrate a low-elaborative or repetitive style; Examples 3 and 4, a high elaborative style.

Example 1: Low Elaborative

Father:	Do you remember who went with us to the beach?
Son:	Wh-
Father:	Who went with us to the beach?
Son:	But we didn't swim too much.
Father:	Mmm hmmm. But we went to the beach. Do you remember who came with us?
Son:	We go. We take food with us. We take food.
Father:	Yeah.
Son:	And a knife. And juice.
Father:	Uh huh. How did we get there?
Son:	( )
Father:	Gosh. How did we get to the beach? Did we drive?
Son:	Yeah.
Father:	Did you like it?
Son:	Yes.

Example 2: Low Elaborative

Father:	So what did you and Nick, what'd you all do at the beach?
Son:	Um, we played sand castles.
Father:	Built sand castles, what else did you do?
Son:	Um, baby was coming here. ((baby brother))
Father:	Um hum.
Son:	And he was coming.
Father:	Mommy was pregnant, that's right.
Son:	He was, he was ( ).
Father:	Did you all do something else?
Son:	I wanna go in there.
Father:	That has to do with a net, remember?

The first two examples reveal the primary hallmark of a parent's low elaborative style: probing the child for a specific piece of information. For instance, in the first example the parent is most interested in getting the child to say with whom they went to the beach. The child responds with a fairly detailed answer about the food they took with them; instead of expanding on this theme, the parent switches topics, after which the child starts responding only minimally. In the second example, also about a trip to the beach, the child responds to the father's questions about their activities but is more interested in talking about the impending arrival of a baby brother. Once again, the parent does not expand on the child's memory of the event but instead returns to his original issue of interest, their activities at the beach. The child quickly loses interest at this point and starts talking about going to see the experimenter in the next room.

Example 3: High Elaborative

Father:	What was fun about the zoo?
Daughter:	Uh. ((pause)) I know what I liked.
Father:	What did you like?
Daughter:	I liked the grillas.
Father:	The gorillas?
Daughter:	Yeah.
Father:	Yeah, we saw some neat gorillas, didn't we?
Daughter:	What do you like?
Father:	Well gee I may—you know that was one of my favorite things. You know, what was, what kind, what kind of gorillas did you like the best?

Daughter:	Ummmm. The black ones.
Father:	The black ones. And, didn't they have some different size gorillas?
Daughter:	I didn't. ( )
Father:	But didn't they have any little baabies?
Daughter:	YEAH!
Father:	What, did they have little baby gorillas?
Daughter:	Yes, I like those. I like those.
Father:	What were they doin'?
Daughter:	They were um, um, eating.
Father:	Eating?

Example 4: High Elaborative

Father:	Do you remember when we went to the seashore with Clifford, and we went for that walk in the woods?
Daughter:	Yeah.
Father:	Yeah? Um, what do you remember about that?
Daughter:	I remember ( ) Clifford.
Father:	Yeah, what was Clifford like? What did he look like?
Daughter:	Um, I don't know.
Father:	Did he have a carrot for a nose?
Daughter:	No.
Father:	Did he have a beard like me?
Daughter:	Yes.
Father:	He's a pretty funny guy, isn't he?

The latter two examples stand in stark contrast to the first two. Note that the children are providing about the same rate of memory information as in the first two excerpts. The most striking difference is in the way parents respond to the children's memories. Parents with high elaborative style follow in and expand on what was most interesting about the event to the child. The end result is that the conversation seems more like a dialogue than like an interrogation on the part of the parent. When parents follow in on children's admittedly minimal responding in this manner, the conversations last longer, and in the process the parent asks a greater number of elaborative questions rather than repeating previous questions which the child is not interested in answering, and which quickly terminate talk about the past event.

Interestingly, in this first study of parental elaboration and children's memory, the results revealed few differences between mothers and fathers in their level of elaboration with their children. Instead, the primary differences were a function of gender of child: Parents were on the whole more elaborative with daughters than with sons. The excerpts discussed earlier focus on parents' differential strategies to similar types of child response patterns. For a variety of reasons, though, we cannot claim from this initial study that parents' greater elaboration with daughters was solely a function of parents' differing gender expectations for daughters and sons. It was also the case in these conversations with children aged 3;4 that girls reported greater amounts of memory information than boys. Therefore, parents' greater elaboration with daughters could be partially or wholly a function of girls' greater participation in the conversations. In other words, it may be that daughters elicit a more elaborative style of responding from their parents than do sons. Because we collected conversations from only one point in time, we could not fully explore the directionality (parent-to-child or child-to-parent) of the elaboration effect. With conversations from more than one point in time and with a variety of partners, we can assess consistency in children's recall over time and across conversational partners, and thus can begin to address the question of whether parents impose a more elaborative style on daughters or if daughters somehow evoke this style from parents (see Bell & Harper, 1977; Russell & Russell, 1992, for further discussion of bidirectionality issues).

The present study is a longitudinal examination of these same children as they reminisce with their mothers and fathers at age 5;10. In looking at parents' contributions to the conversations, the first question for this longitudinal investigation regards differences between mothers and fathers in the way they continue to structure conversations with their children about the past. Although mothers and fathers did not differ from each other in their reminiscing style with their children at age 3;4, it may be the case that any differences between mothers and fathers would be more likely to emerge as children grow older and parents are able to more closely approximate their manner of reminiscing with other adults. Second, even if mothers and fathers retain their similar styles of talking about the past over the preschool period, parents may continue to be more elaborative with daughters than with sons aged 5;10. Previous research indicates an increase in parents' differential treatment of daughters and sons as children grow older (e.g., Block, 1979).

Third, we can examine consistency in children's recall over time. Girls may continue to recall more than boys in conversations with their parents between the ages of 3;6 and 5;10. Children may also exhibit differences in recall as a function of whether they are talking to mothers, fathers, or to someone outside the family sphere. Thus, at each of the two time points, children also discussed memories with a relatively unfamiliar experimenter who provided children with only open-ended prompts. Contrasting children's recall in parent–child conversations with children's recall in independent past narratives provides an even fuller picture of the origins of gender differences in reminiscing. Even if girls experience and respond to a more vivid and detailed style of reminiscing with their parents than do boys, this gender difference may or may not generalize to children's independent recall efforts with less familiar conversational partners. Moreover, through examining children's independent recall with an experimenter at both the early and later time points, we can begin to untangle the relationship between parental elaboration and gender differences in children's recall. If girls independently recall more than boys only at the later time point, it would suggest that parents' early elaborative style with daughters is facilitating girls' later recall with other partners.

Finally, in elucidating possible gender differences in reminiscing among mothers and fathers, daughters and sons, we begin to explore bidirectional influences operating in these conversations. Parents may socialize girls and boys into different styles of reminiscing, but in what ways do children themselves contribute to these emerging gender differences? Through microanalysis of the memory conversations at each time point, we can start to address whether girls and boys respond differently to the same strategies by parents, and whether parents respond differently to similar participation levels of boys and girls.

Thus, the major objectives of the present study are to examine how mothers and fathers talk about the past with daughters and sons across the preschool years and to explore the early emergence of gender differences in autobiographical recall.

METHOD

Subjects

Twenty-four White, middle-class, two-parent families with children aged 3;6 were recruited through county birth records in the Atlanta, Georgia, area for participation in the study. Of this original sample, 17 families completed all relevant tasks at both the 3;6 and 5;10 time points. Two families moved out of state, one family dropped out of the study, and four families had missing data on at least one of the tasks. In 10 of these remaining families, the target child was male; in 7 of the families the target child was female. Seven boys and four girls were firstborns; three boys and three girls were laterborns. All but one father worked full-time outside the home. A majority of the mothers also worked full-time outside the home (58%), with other mothers working part-time (24%) and the remaining mothers working solely inside the home (18%). All parents had attended some college and 80% held a college degree.

Procedure

This study was part of a larger longitudinal project on children's narrative development. One of three female experimenters conducted four sessions in the family's home at each of the following ages: 3;6, 3;10, 4;10, and 5;10. At the outset of the study, experimenters told parents that they were interested in how much and what kind of information children remembered with different conversational partners. Mother–child and experimenter–child memory interviews were conducted during two separate sessions at each of these four time points, and father–child memory interviews were conducted during another session at the 3;6 and 5;10 time points, along with various other tasks.[1] The mother–child interview always occurred before the experimenter–child interview at each time point, but the order of mother–child and father–child interviews was counterbalanced. Within each time point, the three memory interviews were conducted at least 48 hours apart, but within a two- to three-week period.

Event Selection

At all memory interviews, experimenters first aided parents in event selection. Experimenters helped parents select events that had only occurred once and that parents had participated in with children. Events such as birthdays or Christmas were excluded because they tend to be routines even by age 3;6 and children have trouble recalling a specific instance (see Hudson, Fivush, & Kuebli, 1992). The resulting events discussed included visiting the zoo, going to a new amusement park, participating in a wedding, and a host of other unique happenings in the families' lives.[2] The majority of the events discussed were positive and child-centered. Inspection of the transcripts revealed no differences in the kinds of events mothers with daughters and sons and fathers with daughters and sons discussed, other than that only father–son dyads talked about sporting events.

Memory Interviews

After event selection, the parent and child, or experimenter and child, sat comfortably on a couch with the tape recorder between them. In the case of parent–child interviews, parents discussed the past events with their children for as long as they wished. Experimenters were not in the room during parent–child interviews. In experimenter interviews, experimenters introduced each event and asked children to tell as much as they remembered about the event. Experimenters confirmed children's responses and gave nondirective prompts such as "Tell me more about that" or "What else happened?" until children could no longer recall any more about that particular event; then experimenters went on to the next event.

Coding

All memory interviews were transcribed in full in preparation for coding. Then, two coders marked the beginning and ending of discussions about each event. The first three events discussed for which the child remembered at least two unique pieces of information were included in analyses.

The coding scheme for the parent–child interviews, and for the children's responses during the experimenter–child interview, was adapted from a previous coding scheme developed for portions of the same data set (Reese, Haden, & Fivush, 1993). Parent utterances were coded into the following categories.

1. *Elaborations* were parents' questions and statements about the past event that provided a unique piece of information about the event that neither they nor their children had previously mentioned (e.g., child recalls eating ice cream and parent responds, "Ice cream. *It was an ice cream cake. And what was on the ice cream cake?*"; coded as two elaborations).

2. *Repetitions* were parents' questions and statements in which they repeated their own previous question or statement about the event, or the gist of it, without providing any new information (e.g., parent asks "What did we do?" and in the next conversational turn repeats *"Do you remember what we did?"*). Parents' memory prompts (e.g., "Do you remember?" or "Tell me about it") were included as repetitions.

3. *Evaluations* occurred when parents confirmed or negated children's responses by repeating children's utterances along with an explicit evaluation. Within a conversational turn, parents were scored as producing one evaluation for repeating children's utterances in an evaluative context and another for providing purely evaluative words such as "Yeah" or "No" or "That's right, terrific!" Thus, parents could receive a possible total of two evaluations after each child utterance (e.g., child recalls going on the train at the zoo and parent responds by saying, *"Yeah! That's right! We went on the train!"*; coded as two evaluations because the parent included both evaluative types).

4. *Off-topic utterances* consisted of behavioral directives to children or other parent utterances that had nothing to do with the past event in question.

5. *Other utterances* consisted of talk about related past events, comments on the memory process, and unclassifiable utterances.

Children's utterances were coded in the following manner:

1. *Memory responses* were new pieces of information about the event that neither parents nor children had previously mentioned. At times these utterances introduced a completely new topic about the event; other times, these utterances provided new information about a subtopic of the event already being discussed (e.g., parent asks, "Do you remember the rhinoceros?" and child responds with,

"The rhinoceros was running around the man."). Children's genuine memory questions that requested new information were also coded as memory responses (e.g., when discussing her participation in a wedding, child asks, "The kids that weren't anything [in the wedding], could they go swimming?"). Children's memory questions occurred infrequently, at an average of once per event across the two time points.

2. *Memory placeholders* were children's utterances that were not off-topic but that added no new information to the conversation. Sometimes these utterances consisted of children repeating their own or parents' previous utterances (e.g., child says in one turn, "I had a sick throat" and in child's next turn says, *"I was sick"*). At other times, children took a legitimate turn but included no memory information (e.g., "I don't know" or "You tell me.").

3. *Other utterances* by children consisted of their confirmation or negation of parents' utterances, their off-topic comments, and fantasy talk or memory comments that were tangential to the past event discussion.

For the experimenter–child interview, only children's memory responses were coded. That is, children received credit for each proposition containing a new piece of information. The memory placeholder category was not relevant to the experimenter–child interviews and was not coded. Because the experimenter contributed only open-ended prompts in the experimenter–child memory interviews, these were not conversations; in this interview situation the child could not appropriately repeat their own or the experimenter's previous memory utterance but provide no new memory information. For parents' elaborations, repetitions, and for children's memory responses in all interviews, the unit of coding was the subject–verb proposition. For parent evaluations, the unit of coding was the type of evaluation, as described earlier. Children's memory placeholders in the parent–child interviews were only coded when there were no other codeable utterances in the conversational turn. Thus, children could only receive a possible total of one memory placeholder for each conversational turn.

Reliability on parent and child utterances in the parent–child interviews ranged from 82% to 90% across the two time points. For the experimenter–child interviews, reliability on children's memory responses ranged from 86% to 99% across the two time points.

RESULTS

Results are presented in three major sections. Analyses focus first on whether mothers and fathers differ from each other and with their daughters and sons in their use of elaborations, evaluations, repetitions, or off-topic talk over the preschool years. The next analysis examines patterns of difference in girls' and boys' responses in memory conversations with their mothers, fathers, and independent narratives with an experimenter. Because the results of these analyses reveal interesting gender differences, a third set of analyses was conducted to provide a more fine-grained examination of parental replies to children's responses in these memory conversations. Specifically, differences by gender of parent and gender of child are determined within the memory conversations for parents' and children's contingent responding.

Because a few children at each time point (though never the same child across time points) did not recall all three events in these conversations with their mothers, fathers, and experimenters,[3] we chose to sum the occurrence of codes across events and average them rather than use totals. Thus, analyses were based on mean frequencies of each utterance type per past event.

Differences in Mothers' and Fathers' Talk With Daughters and Sons Over Time

The first question concerns possible differences by gender of parent and gender of child in the types of utterances used by mothers and fathers in memory conversations with their daughters and sons over time. More specifically, of interest were differences between mothers and fathers in their overall use of elaborations, evaluations, repetitions, and off-topic talk, and how mothers' and fathers' use of these conversational codes might also differ with daughters and sons at ages 3;6 and 5;10. Mean frequencies (and standard deviations) per event for mothers' and fathers' use of elaborations, evaluations, repetitions, and off-topic talk, as well as total number of utterances, by gender of child and time are displayed in Table 1.

A preliminary analysis was conducted on the mean number of the total utterance codes per event for each mother and each father, as an

TABLE 1
Mean Frequencies (and Standard Deviations) Per Event of Mothers' and Fathers' Utterance
Types by Gender of Child and Time

Utterance Type	Mother				Father			
	Daughter		Son		Daughter		Son	
Elaborations								
3;6	20.11	(10.11)	17.68	(4.46)	26.67	(11.67)	16.39	(8.41)
5;10	24.67	(9.73)	19.53	(11.06)	27.00	(10.33)	28.03	(17.81)
Evaluations								
3;6	13.83	(9.67)	8.47	(3.58)	15.48	(6.15)	10.07	(5.28)
5;10	16.29	(10.75)	7.72	(5.42)	12.00	(6.81)	16.55	(11.79)
Repetitions								
3;6	10.55	(4.42)	10.45	(4.12)	13.31	(12.49)	8.23	(5.34)
5;10	7.33	(3.63)	7.33	(5.17)	7.95	(4.04)	12.45	(10.81)
Off-topic talk								
3;6	5.17	(2.69)	4.70	(4.10)	2.26	(2.28)	3.53	(3.02)
5;10	1.62	(2.21)	2.75	(6.20)	0.38	(0.49)	2.65	(4.88)
Total utterances								
3;6	54.42	(25.44)	44.75	(12.45)	62.91	(29.72)	41.10	(19.19)
5;10	56.62	(30.69)	44.37	(29.34)	58.57	(21.47)	67.02	(49.74)

average measure of the conversational length per event for each parent. A 2 (time point) by 2 (gender of child) by 2 (gender of parent) analysis of variance (ANOVA) performed on this measure revealed that mothers and fathers did not differ in the length of their conversations with their children at either of the two time points. However, fathers increase over time in their total utterances with sons, but not with daughters; mothers' conversational length with daughters and sons does not increase over time, $F(1,15) = 3.90$, $p = .06$.

An overall 2 (time point) by 2 (gender of child) by 2 (gender of parent) by 4 (conversational code: elaborations, evaluations, repetitions, off-topic) ANOVA was next conducted with time point, gender of parent, and conversational code as within-subject factors and gender of child as a between-subject factor. Results revealed a marginally significant 4-way interaction ($F(3,45) = 2.48$, $p = .07$), as well a 3-way interaction of gender of child by gender of parent by time ($F(1,15) = 6.86$, $p < .02$), 2-way interactions of time by conversational code ($F(3,45) = 6.05$, $p < .001$), and gender of parent by conversational code ($F(3,45) = 2.36$, $p = .08$), and a main effect of conversational code ($F(3,45) = 92.33$, $p < .001$). To explore these effects in detail, analyses were conducted separately for each conversational code by time, gender of child, and gender of parent, and followed up by post-hoc tests where appropriate.

For elaborations, a 2 (time point) by 2 (gender of child) by 2 (gender of parent) ANOVA, with time point and gender of parent as within-subject factors and gender of child as a between-subject factor, was conducted. There was a tendency for both mothers and fathers to use a greater frequency of elaborations with daughters ($M = 23.39$) than with sons ($M = 17.02$) at the 3;6 time point, but no differences by gender of child or parent at 5;10 ($M = 25.83$ with daughters; $M = 23.78$ with sons), $F(1, 15) = 6.86$, $p = .07$. However, as can be seen in the table, fathers use fewer elaborations with their sons at the first time point, compared with fathers' use of elaborations with sons at the last time point, and with mothers' elaborations with sons over time.

A 2 (time point) by 2 (gender of child) by 2 (gender of parent) ANOVA was conducted for mothers' and fathers' use of evaluations. At both time points, mothers were providing significantly more evaluations with daughters than with sons; fathers with daughters also use significantly more evaluations than fathers with sons at age 3;6, but no differences for fathers emerged at the 5;10 time point, $F(1,15) = 6.20$, $p < .05$.

A 2 (time point) by 2 (gender of child) by 2 (gender of parent) ANOVA indicated no differences by gender of child or parent for mothers' and fathers' repetitions at child's age 3;6, but with a child aged 5;10 fathers were using more repetitions ($M = 10.60$) than mothers ($M = 7.33$); particularly, fathers with sons were using more repetitions than fathers with daughters, $F(1,15) = 4.86$, $p = <.05$.

A 2 (time point) by 2 (gender of child) by 2 (gender of parent) ANOVA for off-topic utterances yielded no significant main effects of time point, gender of child or parent, and no interactions.

Surprisingly then despite the research that has found differences in adult females' and males' autobiographical memory reports, these results indicate very few differences between mothers and fathers in the ways they talk about the past with their preschool children. Although fathers were found to be more repetitive than mothers at the later time point, especially with sons, mothers and fathers did not differ from each other in their use of elaborations, evaluations, off-topic comments, or length of the memory conversations with their children over time.

Where we do find differences is by gender of child; parent–daughter conversations about the past are different from parent–son conversations. Particularly at the earlier time point, mothers and fathers are more evaluative and somewhat more elaborative in talking about the past with their daughters than are mothers and fathers with sons. Elaborations provide more detailed information about the event under discussion and may help to cue the child's memory, enabling the child to access and contribute more memory information to the recount. Evaluations give explicit feedback, acknowledgment, and frequently praise the child's participation in the conversation. In this way, the finding that parents with daughters are providing more evaluations and somewhat more elaborations during memory conversations than parents with sons is consistent with the idea that very early, females are being socialized to tell richly detailed, embellished stories about the past, and to view reminiscing as a valued way of interacting socially with others.

Clearly though, care must be taken in interpreting these results with regard to directionality of effect. In fact, these findings of differences in parents' talk by gender of child are even more provocative in light of the children's contributions to the memory conversations to which we now turn.

Children's Talk With Mothers, Fathers, and Experimenters Over Time

As stated earlier, children's provision of unique memory information was coded in memory conversations with the mother, father, and experimenter at both time points. To determine possible gender differences in preschoolers' mean frequency of memory responses per event, a 2 (time point) by 2 (gender of child) by 3 (partner: mother, father, experimenter) ANOVA was conducted, with time point and partner as within-subjects factors and gender of child as a between-subjects factor. As can be seen in Figure 1, for both boys and girls and across partner, provision of memory responses increased significantly over time, $F(1,15) = 40.74, p < .001$. However, across time and partner, girls were providing significantly more memory information than boys, $F(1,15) = 8.22, p < .01$. Interestingly, a main effect of partner was also found, such that both boys and girls were providing more memory responses with their fathers than with either their mothers or experimenters over time, $F(2,30) = 4.71, p < .02$.

In the mother–child and father–child conversations about the past

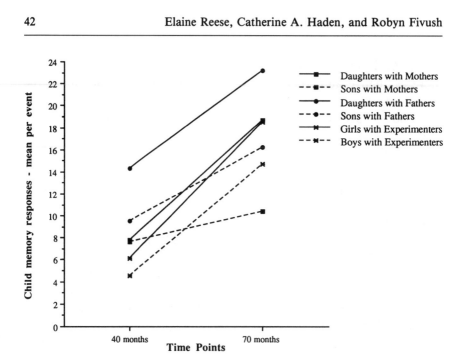

FIGURE 1   Mean frequencies per event of children's memory responses with mother, father, and experimenter over time.

at both time points, instances when the girls' and boys' responses in the conversation provided no new memory information were also coded; as noted earlier, memory placeholders were not relevant in the experimenter–child interviews. For children's memory placeholders, a 2 (time point) by 2 (gender of child) by 2 (gender of parent) ANOVA revealed no main effects of time, gender of child or parent, and no interactions.

Thus, children are generally recalling more memory information over time with all partners. Further, there were no differences for girls' and boys' provision of memory placeholders by gender of child, gender of parent, or time. However, boys and girls are providing more memory responses in conversations with their fathers than with their mothers or experimenters. Most intriguing, girls are providing more memory responses than boys with their mothers, fathers, and in independent past event narratives with an experimenter across the preschool period. Thus, very early in development, girls are contributing more detailed memory information than boys with different partners, including an experimenter who uses only open-ended prompts. Girls' provision of more memory responses is not simply a function of differences in parents' talk to daughters and sons, but generalizes to unfamiliar conversational partners as well.

Yet, perhaps it is not surprising that girls are recounting more memory information than boys, based on the finding that mothers and fathers are more elaborative and evaluative with daughters than with sons. Quite possibly, girls are learning the skills of remembering in parent–child conversations and these skills generalize to other conversational partners as well. In order to examine the relationships between parents' and children's talk about the past in more detail, we conducted contingency analyses of parent and child utterances.

Mothers' and Fathers' Replies to Daughters' and Sons' Responses in Memory Conversations

Here we take a microanalytic approach to understanding factors contributing to gender differences in preschoolers' autobiographical memories. To further address the origin of girls' greater recall in conversations, we first examine whether parents reply differently to boys' and girls' responses. Next, we assess whether girls and boys respond differently to similar parental strategies. The first set of contingency analyses focused on parents' replies to children. We first asked whether mothers and fathers are more likely to reply with a particular utterance type to their daughters' and sons' memory responses, and second, how those replies might differ by gender of parent, gender of child, and time.

To give some examples of these child response–parent contingent reply relationships, mothers and fathers could reply with elaborations following daughters' and sons' memory responses or memory placeholders:[4]

Example 5

Father:	Do you remember what shoes we wore?	
Daughter:	Watershoes.	MEMORY RESPONSE
Father:	What was fun about the water shoes?	ELABORATION

Example 6

Mother:	Where were our seats?	
Son:	Um, I forgot.	PLACEHOLDER
Mother:	Wa:::y up high.	ELABORATION
	How high?	ELABORATION

Mothers and fathers could instead reply with evaluations following daughters' and sons' memory responses or memory placeholders.

Example 7

Mother:	Do you remember what we did on Christmas when we went to Bermuda?	
Daughter:	We went to the beach.	MEMORY RESPONSE
Mother:	We sure did.	EVALUATION

For these analyses we further considered mothers' and fathers' replies of repetitions or off-topic talk following daughters' and sons' memory responses and memory placeholders, as in:

Example 8

Mother:	And so what did we do with the lights off?	
Daughter:	I can't see anything in the dark.	MEMORY RESPONSE
Mother:	No.	EVALUATION
	So what did we do?	REPETITION

Therefore, in these analyses, conditional probabilities of mothers' and fathers' elaborations, evaluations, repetitions, and off-topic talk in reply to daughters' and sons' memory responses and memory placeholders were calculated. That is, given that the daughter or son provided a memory response, what proportion of the mother's and father's contingent utterances were elaborations, evaluations, repetitions, and off-topic talk? And given that the daughter or son provided a memory placeholder, what proportion of the mother's and father's contingent utterances were elaborations, evaluations, repetitions, and off-topic talk?

Tables 2 and 3 show the conditional probabilities of mothers' and fathers' reply types to girls' and boys' memory responses and memory placeholders respectively at each time point. Separate 2 (time point) by 2 (gender of child) by 2 (gender of parent) ANOVAs were performed on

TABLE 2
Conditional Probabilities of Mothers' and Fathers' Replies Following Daughters' and Sons'
Memory Responses Over Time

Parents' Replies	Mother				Father			
	Daughter		Son		Daughter		Son	
Elaborations								
3;6	.50	(.10)	.55	(.20)	.63	(.12)	.52	(.13)
5;10	.62	(.15)	.62	(.22)	.59	(.10)	.54	(.17)
Evaluations								
3;6	.34	(.09)	.25	(.11)	.26	(.11)	.34	(.16)
5;10	.29	(.12)	.20	(.11)	.31	(.07)	.31	(.16)
Repetitions								
3;6	.11	(.05)	.16	(.11)	.09	(.08)	.08	(.06)
5;10	.07	(.05)	.09	(.08)	.06	(.06)	.08	(.05)
Off-topic talk								
3;6	.00	(.00)	.01	(.02)	.02	(.03)	.01	(.03)
5;10	.00	(.00)	.01	(.04)	.01	(.01)	.02	(.02)

TABLE 3
Conditional Probabilities of Mothers' and Fathers' Replies Following Daughters' and Sons'
Memory Placeholders Over Time

Parents' Replies	Mother				Father			
	Daughter		Son		Daughter		Son	
Elaborations								
3;6	.55	(.10)	.60	(.15)	.57	(.10)	.54	(.09)
5;10	.61	(.13)	.69	(.18)	.65	(.08)	.61	(.17)
Evaluations								
3;6	.14	(.09)	.08	(.07)	.08	(.10)	.15	(.09)
5;10	.16	(.07)	.07	(.05)	.10	(.08)	.10	(.07)
Repetitions								
3;6	.25	(.06)	.30	(.09)	.28	(.12)	.23	(.07)
5;10	.15	(.09)	.16	(.11)	.15	(.08)	.21	(.11)
Off-topic talk								
3;6	.01	(.04)	.01	(.02)	.02	(.04)	.03	(.04)
5;10	.02	(.04)	.01	(.04)	.04	(.05)	.02	(.02)

each of the eight types of conditional probabilities.[5] As shown in Table 2, mothers' elaboration replies to daughters' and sons' memory responses increased over time, whereas fathers showed no change in elaboration replies over time, $F(1,15) = 4.02$, $p = .06$. For evaluation replies to children's memory responses, mothers in interactions with daughters were more likely to reply with evaluations than mothers in interactions with sons, whereas fathers in interactions with daughters were equally likely to reply with evaluations as fathers in interactions with sons over time, $F(1,15) = 5.15$, $p < .05$. Also shown in Table 2, fathers were more likely than mothers to reply to a son's memory response with an evaluation. Both mothers and fathers use fewer repetition replies to daughters' and sons' memory responses over time, $F(1,15) = 7.40$, $p < .02$. There were no significant effects of time, gender of child, or gender of parent for mothers' and fathers' off-topic replies to girls' and boys' memory responses.

As displayed in Table 3, in replies to daughters' and sons' memory placeholders, mothers and fathers increased significantly in elaboration replies, $F(1,15) = 8.41$, $p < .01$, and decreased in repetition replies over time, $F(1,15) = 27.00$, $p < .001$. Mothers interacting with daughters were more likely to reply with evaluations of child memory placeholders than were mothers interacting with sons, whereas between the dyads of fathers and daughters and of fathers and sons there was no difference, $F(1,15) = 10.46$, $p < .01$. Also, mothers interacting with daughters were more likely to reply with evaluations to child memory placeholders than fathers interacting with daughters, whereas fathers speaking with sons were more likely to use evaluations than mothers with their sons. No significant effects of time, gender of child, or gender of parent were revealed for mothers' and fathers' off-topic replies to girls' and boys' memory placeholders.

Overall, these analyses again reveal few differences between mothers and fathers in their contingent replies of elaborations, repetitions, and off-topic comments to either their children's memory responses or memory placeholders. In particular, whereas mothers, but not fathers, increase in their elaboration replies to daughters' and sons' memory responses over time, mothers and fathers both increase in elaboration replies to sons' and daughters' memory placeholders. Both mothers and fathers decrease in repetition replies to daughters' and sons' memory responses and memory placeholders over time.

Importantly, though, evaluation replies show effects of both gender of parent and gender of child. In particular, there is a greater distinction between mother–daughter and mother–son conversations than between father–daughter and father–son conversations following children's memory responses and memory placeholders. Mothers are more likely to reply with evaluations to daughters' memory responses and placeholders than are mothers to sons' memory responses and placeholders, whereas fathers show no such differences. Whether contributing more memory information or simply showing a willingness to participate in the conversations, girls are receiving more explicit feedback from their mothers about their contributions than are boys. Interestingly, however, sons' memory responses and placeholders are evaluated more by their fathers than by their mothers. Thus, for evaluation replies to children's responses in the memory conversations, there is an indication of differentiation between mothers and fathers when talking with the child of their same gender.

Girls' and Boys' Replies to Mothers' and Fathers' Utterances in Memory Conversations

A second set of contingency analyses examined children's responses to parents' utterances. When parents gave an elaboration in a conversational turn, what proportion of children's replies were memory responses versus memory placeholders? Children's contingent replies were also calculated in response to parents' repetitions and evaluations. Children infrequently gave on-topic (either memory or placeholder) replies to parents' off-topic utterances, and therefore these contingencies were not analyzed. Examples 9–11 demonstrate some of these contingent relationships.

Children could reply with a memory response after a parent elaboration, repetition, or evaluation.

Example 9

Mother:	((second request)) Tell me what you remember	
	about Marineland.	REPETITION
Son:	We saw dolphins.	MEMORY RESPONSE

Example 10

Mother:	We went to see the stables where she goes	
	horseback riding	
Daughter:	Yeah.	
Mother:	Yeah.	EVALUATION
Daughter:	I pet them on the nose!	MEMORY RESPONSE

Or, children could respond with a memory placeholder after a parent elaboration, repetition, or evaluation.

Example 11

Father:	Yeah, what was Clifford like?	ELABORATION
	What did he look like?	ELABORATION
Daughter:	Um, I don't know.	MEMORY PLACEHOLDER

   Separate 2 (time point) by 2 (gender of child) by 2 (gender of parent) ANOVAs were performed on each of the six types of conditional probabilities. Table 4 shows the conditional probabilities of girls' and boys' memory responses to mothers' and fathers' elaborations, repetitions, and evaluations at each time point. Children increased their provision of memory responses to all of these parent utterance types over time (after elaborations, $F(1,15) = 18.55$, $p < .01$; after repetitions, $F(1,15) = 10.06$, $p < .01$; after evaluations, $F(1,15) = 8.73$, $p < .01$). Children in some instances responded differentially based on parent gender. First, children were more likely to give a memory response after a father's elaboration than after a mother's, $F(1,15) = 5.72$, $p < .05$. Second, girls tended to respond to more father repetitions with a memory reply, whereas boys tended to respond to more mother repetitions with a memory reply, $F(1,15) = 4.06$, $p = .06$.
   Table 5 shows the conditional probabilities of girls' and boys' memory placeholders contingent upon mothers' and fathers' elaborations, repetitions, and evaluations. Again, effects of age were apparent. Children decreased their memory placeholder responses after parents' elaborations, $F(1,15) = 5.76$, $p < .05$, and evaluations, $F(1,15) = 5.89$, $p < .05$. Marginal effects by parent and child gender were also observed

TABLE 4

Conditional Probabilities of Daughters' and Sons' Memory Responses to Mothers' and Fathers' Utterances Over Time

| | Daughter | | | | Son | | | |
Parents' Utterances	Mother		Father		Mother		Father	
Elaborations								
3;6	.28	(.07)	.45	(.17)	.33	(.15)	.40	(.10)
5;10	.50	(.10)	.58	(.19)	.43	(.10)	.46	(.14)
Evaluations								
3;6	.28	(.14)	.46	(.32)	.27	(.18)	.36	(.26)
5;10	.49	(.19)	.49	(.16)	.48	(.29)	.52	(.28)
Repetitions								
3;6	.20	(.13)	.37	(.20)	.37	(.22)	.30	(.19)
5;10	.38	(.14)	.55	(.21)	.52	(.29)	.41	(.27)

TABLE 5
Conditional Probabilities of Daughters' and Sons' Memory Placeholders to Mothers' and
Fathers' Utterances Over Time

Parents' Utterances	Daughter				Son			
	Mother		Father		Mother		Father	
Elaborations								
3;6	.60	(.19)	.49	(.16)	.53	(.19)	.50	(.12)
5;10	.42	(.09)	.35	(.16)	.51	(.09)	.47	(.14)
Evaluations								
3;6	.54	(.17)	.47	(.33)	.49	(.18)	.52	(.28)
5;10	.37	(.10)	.42	(.16)	.40	(.33)	.35	(.23)
Repetitions								
3;6	.52	(.21)	.52	(.27)	.46	(.18)	.52	(.19)
5;10	.58	(.16)	.42	(.18)	.44	(.26)	.47	(.30)

after parents' elaborations: Girls tended to give fewer placeholders after parent elaborations than boys at the latter time point only, $F(1,15) = 3.26$, $p = .09$; and children were slightly less likely to give a placeholder after a father's elaboration than after a mother's, $F(1,15) = 3.13$, $p = .10$.

These analyses of the way children respond to parent utterances demonstrate that children are more responsive to all types of parents' on-task utterances over time in their use of more memory responses and fewer placeholders. Children also seem to be responding differentially to some extent based on parent gender. They are more responsive to fathers' elaborations than mothers', and there was some tendency for girls to be more responsive to fathers' repetitions and for boys to be more responsive to mothers' repetitions. Across partners, girls had a slight tendency to be more responsive than boys, but only at the later time point. This is not the pattern we would expect if girls were eliciting higher levels of elaboration and evaluation from parents than were boys. If this were the case, then we would expect girls to show higher levels of responsiveness to both mothers and fathers than do boys, especially at the earlier time point, when the parental differences are most acute. Across analyses of conversational patterns, parents respond differentially to daughters' and sons' utterances, but girls and boys do not respond differentially to parents' utterances. This pattern, although only suggestive, supports the interpretation that children are responding to differential socialization of reminiscing from parents more than parents are responding to existing gender differences in children.

DISCUSSION

In contrast to accumulating reports that women recount richer past experiences and recall more memories from early childhood than do men (e.g., Ross & Holmberg, 1990; Mullen, 1994), these results present very little evidence to support the notion that mothers and fathers differ dramatically in their style of reminiscing with their children. However, we did find pervasive and enduring gender differences, both in the ways daughters and sons recalled past events, and in the ways parents reminisce differently with daughters and sons in these conversations.

Across the 30-month period of study, mothers and fathers did not differ from each other in the overall level of new information they provided about past events for their children, or in their overall evaluations of children's utterances and off-topic comments. These findings of marked similarities between mothers and fathers were unexpected given other findings of differences in men's and women's reminiscing. That men and women talk about the past in similar ways to their children across the preschool period suggests that adult gender differences in reminiscing may be dependent on the context in which the discussion takes place and the partner with whom the memory is being recalled. Previous studies of gender differences in reminiscing have most often taken place in the laboratory, and always with an experimenter questioning the respondent (e.g., Cowan & Davidson, 1984; Ross & Holmberg, 1990; Friedman & Pines, 1991). In contrast, in our study, mothers and fathers reminisced in their own homes and with an intimate partner—their child. Moreover, mothers and fathers engaged in *conversations* with their children, in which parents and children jointly recounted experiences they shared together in the past, as opposed to an experimenter eliciting recall from an "experimental subject." Any or all of these aspects of the context of recalling personal past events may be contributing to the differences in findings. When the context is more familiar, intimate, and relational, men and women may appear similar to each other in their conversational style of talking about the past (see Fivush & Reese, 1992, for an extension of this argument).

However, differential parental treatment according to child gender was marked, and these patterns were somewhat different for mothers and fathers. Whereas parents adopted a more evaluative style overall with daughters than with sons, and were more elaborative with daughters than sons at the 3;6 time point, contingency analyses revealed several ways in which gender of parent and gender of child interacted. Over time, mothers, but not fathers, increased in their elaboration replies to daughters' and sons' memory responses (see Reese et al., 1993, for more extended discussion of maternal elaborations over time). And mothers were more likely to reply with evaluations to daughters' memory responses and memory placeholders than mothers replying to sons, with no such differentiation for fathers. Overall, fathers were more repetitive than mothers at the last time point, particularly in their interactions with sons; fathers were also more likely to reply to sons' memory responses with an evaluation than were mothers.

In general, then, fathers of daughters and fathers of sons were not as different in the way they replied to their children's utterances as were mothers of daughters and mothers of sons. At least in this regard, mothers appear to be differentiating more on the basis of child gender than are fathers, a finding that is at odds with most previous research on parents' gender-stereotyped expectations and play behavior. Most studies that indicate a difference in gender typing between mothers and fathers have found that fathers gender type children to a greater extent than do mothers (see Block, 1983, and Lytton & Romney, 1991, for reviews). One possible reason for this discrepancy is that previous research has focused primarily on parents' differential play behavior with their children. Mothers and fathers may engage in more or less gender typing of their children depending on the degree to which they value the activity. Fathers, more than mothers, take on the role of playmate with their children (e.g., Clarke-Stewart, 1980); it may be that mothers engage in reminiscing and conversing more often with their children and place more importance on the activity than do fathers. In accord with theories of gender- and self-schemas (e.g., Markus, Crane, Bernstein, & Siladi, 1982), greater parental gender typing may occur for those activities that are highly valued and are thus more salient to the particular parent. If women value reminiscing more highly than men (Ross & Holmberg, 1990), the ability to talk fluently about past events may be a more salient part of the self-concept, and ultimately of gender identity, for mothers than for fathers (see Fivush & Reese, 1992, for related arguments).

Most important, the finding that parents differentially respond according to gender of child supports the notion that girls are receiving early and continued feedback that reminiscing is a valued activity. Both mothers and fathers also modeled for girls more than boys the specific forms of an elaborative style in the process of talking about the past, especially in the early preschool period. Implicitly and explicitly, parents are informing their daughters of the forms and functions of reminiscing. Interestingly, socialization of reminiscing appears to be especially strong within same-sex dyads. In response to their memory-relevant utterances, sons received greater praise from their fathers than from their mothers, and daughters received greater praise from their mothers than from their fathers. This finding may reflect the more general tendency for parents to focus their socialization efforts more intensely onto their same-sex children (see Fagot, 1974).

Evidence of gender socialization by parents must be considered in light of what are certainly bidirectional influences operating between parents and children. Striking differences were found between boys and girls even by the beginning of the preschool years. Girls consistently recalled more unique information in the conversations than boys, across the preschool period and regardless of conversational partner. This finding provides dramatic evidence for the early emergence of adult gender differences in reminiscing, and once again brings up the question of whether parents' greater elaboration with daughters is simply a function of girls' greater recall.

The contingency analysis of boys' and girls' responding to parent utterances, however, revealed little evidence to support this notion that girls are simply eliciting an elaborative style from parents in their early reminiscing. Girls and boys showed no initial differences in their responsiveness to various parental strategies. Instead, girls became marginally more responsive than boys at the later time point, again providing support for parental socialization explanations of girls' reminiscing. Clearly, research with children even younger than age 3 is necessary before we can draw any firm conclusions about the origins of these gender differences.

A final, unexpected finding in this study was that both boys and girls recalled more when talking about the past with their fathers than with their mothers or an experimenter. Because there were very few obtained differences between mothers and fathers, and particularly because there were no differences between mothers' and fathers' conversational length, we cannot explain this finding on the basis of different ways that fathers and mothers were conversing with the children. Instead, these findings lead us once again to the role of children in shaping their own early interactions. For the families in this study, mothers performed the role of primary caretaker. Talking about the past with their fathers, or simply having the chance to spend time alone with their fathers, may have been a special event for these children. Indeed, even though the events that mothers and fathers selected to discuss were similar, events experienced with fathers may have been marked by children as more unique than those experienced with mothers, simply by virtue of the children spending less time with their fathers. Both of these aspects may have contributed to children's greater recall with fathers. Future research might address frequency differences in mother–child and father–child reminiscing, as well as the distinctiveness of events discussed with mothers and with fathers. Comparing children's independent recall for events experienced with mothers only and fathers only would be one way of testing this hypothesis.

Regardless of the ultimate explanation of why children recall more with fathers than other conversational partners, the results of this study clearly establish that gender differences in autobiographical recall emerge surprisingly early in development. Both mothers and fathers provide more elaborations and evaluations with daughters than with sons, especially in the early preschool period. Moreover, there is some indication that mothers are replying with more elaborations and evaluations of their daughters' memory responses than their sons', and this may be among the factors contributing to this gender difference. However, it must be stressed that gender differences in autobiographical recall, especially in adults, seem to be quite context sensitive. When reminiscing in the privacy of their home, with their own children, the fathers' recounts are just as elaborative and detailed as the mothers'. Thus, whereas this study documents developmentally early gender differences in reminiscing, it at the same time underscores the flexibility of these differences in social interactions.

NOTES

1   At each time point some events were discussed only by the mother, father, or experimenter, and some events were discussed by either the mother and the experimenter or the mother and the father. However, as this was not the focus of this study and all measures were calculated as mean per event, this factor was not included in the analysis.

2 Other tasks consisted of mother–child free play, mother–child storybook reading, mother–child photograph viewing, a self-concept measure for children, and children's literacy measures.

3 Six dyads at the 3;6 time point (three mother–child pairs and three father–child pairs) and three dyads at the 5;10 time point (one mother–child pair and two father–child pairs) had only two codeable events. Importantly, these were different parents at each time point.

4 In the contingency analyses, mothers' and fathers' elaborations included an elaboration-only reply or an evaluation-plus-elaboration reply sequence following their children's memory response or memory placeholder. Similarly, mothers' and fathers' repetition replies included a repetition-only or evaluation-plus-repetition sequence.

5 We are aware that there is currently a debate in the literature about the most appropriate statistical technique for analyzing contingency data. However, we believe parametric tests are appropriate for several reasons. First, although it is true that each conditional probability by itself is a categorical variable, it is also the case that each participant's conditional probability can vary from 0 to 1. Therefore, the conditional probabilities do form a continuous variable, and analysis of variance is an appropriate procedure. Second, although some statisticians recommend logistic regression for these kinds of data, given our small sample size, this was not a viable option. Finally, previous research in this area has used analysis of variance to analyze contingent responses, and in order for these results to be comparable to already published accounts, analysis of variance seemed the most appropriate technique.

REFERENCES

Bell, R. Q., & Harper, L. V. (1977). *Child effects on adults.* Hillsdale, NJ: Lawrence Erlbaum Associates, Inc.

Block, J. H. (1979). Another look at sex differentiation in the socialization behavior of mothers and fathers. In J. Sherman & F. L. Denmark (Eds.), *Psychology of women: Future directions of research* (pp. 29–87). New York: Psychological Dimensions.

Block, J. H. (1983). Differential premises arising from differential socialization of the sexes: Some conjectures. *Child Development, 54,* 1335–1354.

Clarke-Stewart, K. A. (1980). The father's contribution to children's cognitive and social development in early childhood. In F. A. Pedersen (Ed.), *The father-infant relationship: Observational studies in a family setting* (pp. 111–146). New York: Praeger.

Cowan, N., & Davidson, G. (1984). Salient childhood memories. *Journal of Genetic Psychology, 145,* 101–107.

Eisenberg, A. R. (1985). Learning to describe past experiences in conversation. *Discourse Processes, 8,* 177–204.

Engel, S. (1986, April). *The role of mother–child interaction in autobiographical recall.* In J. A. Hudson (Chair), Learning to talk about the past. Symposium conducted at the Southeastern Conference on Human Development, Nashville, TN.

Fagot, B. I. (1974). Sex differences in toddlers' behavior and parental reaction. *Developmental Psychology, 10,* 554–558.

Fivush, R., Haden, C., & Reese, E. (in press). Remembering, recounting and reminiscing: The development of autobiographical memory in social context. In D. C. Rubin (Ed.), *Reconstructing our past: An overview of autobiographical memory.* Cambridge, England: Cambridge University Press.

Fivush, R., & Reese, E. (1992). The social construction of autobiographical memory. In M. A. Conway, D. C. Rubin, H. Spinnler, & W. A. Wagenaar (Eds.), *Theoretical perspectives on autobiographical memory* (pp. 115–132). The Netherlands: Kluwer.

Friedman, A., & Pines, A. (1991). Sex differences in gender-related childhood memories. *Sex Roles, 25,* 25–32.

Galotti, K. M., Kozberg, S. F., & Farmer, M. C. (1991). Gender and developmental differences in adolescents' conceptions of moral reasoning. *Journal of Youth and Adolescence, 20,* 13–30.

Gilligan, C. (1982). *In a different voice: Psychological theory and women's development.* Cambridge, MA: Harvard University Press.

Hudson, J. A. (1990). The emergence of autobiographic memory in mother–child conversation. In R. Fivush & J. A. Hudson (Eds.), *Knowing and remembering in young children* (pp. 166–196). Cambridge, England: Cambridge University Press.

Hudson, J. A., Fivush, R., & Kuebli, J. (1992). Scripts and episodes: The development of event memory. *Applied Cognitive Psychology, 6,* 483–505.

Johnson, C. (1994). Gender, legitimate authority, and leader–subordinate conversations. *American Sociological Review, 59,* 122–135.

Lytton, H., & Romney, D. M. (1991). Parents' differential socialization of boys and girls: A meta-analysis. *Psychological Bulletin, 109,* 267–296.

Markus, H., Crane, M., Bernstein, S., & Siladi, M. (1982). Self-schemas and gender. *Journal of Personality and Social Psychology, 42,* 38–50.

Middleton, D., & Edwards, D. (1990). Conversational remembering: A social psychological approach. In D. Middleton & D. Edwards (Eds.), *Collective remembering* (pp. 23–45). London, England: Sage.

Miller, P. J., Potts, R., Fung, H., Hoogstra, L., & Mintz, J. (1990). Narrative practices and the social construction of self in childhood. *American Ethnologist, 17,* 292–311.

Miller, P. J., & Sperry (1988). Early talk about the past: The origins of conversational stories of personal experience. *Journal of Child Language, 15,* 293–315.

Mullen, M. K. (1994). Earliest recollections of childhood: A demographic analysis. *Cognition, 52,* 55–79.

Nelson, K. (1993). The psychological and social origins of autobiographical memory. *Psychological Science, 1,* 1–8.

Pillemer, D., & White, S. H. (1989). Childhood events recalled by children and adults. *Advances in Child Development and Behavior, 21,* 297–340.

Reese, E., & Fivush, R. (1993). Parental styles of talking about the past. *Developmental Psychology, 29,* 596–606.

Reese, E., Haden, C. A., & Fivush, R. (1993). Mother–child conversations about the past: Relationships of style and memory over time. *Cognitive Development, 8,* 403–430.

Ross, M., & Holmberg, D. (1990). Recounting the past: Gender differences in the recall of events in the history of a close relationship. In M. P. Zanna & J. M. Olson (Eds.), *The Ontario Symposium: Vol. 6. Self-inference processes* (pp. 135–152). Hillsdale, NJ: Lawrence Erlbaum Associates, Inc.

Russell, A., & Russell, G. (1992). Child effects on socialization research: Some conceptual and data analysis issues. *Social Development, 1,* 163–184.

Sachs, J. (1983). Talking about the there and then: The emergence of displaced reference in parent–child discourse. In K. Nelson (Ed.), *Children's language* (Vol. 4, pp. 1–28). Hillsdale, NJ: Lawrence Erlbaum Associates, Inc.

Tannen, D. (1990). Gender differences in topical coherence: Creating involvement in best friend's talk. *Discourse Processes, 13,* 73–90.

Research on Language and Social Interaction, 29(1), 57–80

You Can Be the Baby Brother, But You Aren't Born Yet: Preschool Girls' Negotiation for Power and Access in Pretend Play

Amy Sheldon
Department of Speech-Communication
University of Minnesota

. . . . that's how you know you belong, if the stories incorporate you into them.

Leslie Marmon Silko. *Storyteller.*

GENDER, CONFLICT, AND LANGUAGE

Developing skills for managing conflict in everyday social interactions is a central achievement in childhood, as well as an ongoing

This article is part of a larger study of gender differences in preschoolers' conversations. Support for this project was provided by the University of Minnesota through a Graduate School Grant-in-Aid, a McKnight Fellowship in the Arts and Humanities, a Summer Faculty Research Grant, a grant from the Conflict and Change Center, and a small grant from the Center for Research in Learning, Perception and Cognition. Sara Hayden and Diane Johnson provided research assistance. I am grateful to the children and parents who participated in this study as well as for generous assistance given by the staff at the University of Minnesota Child Care Center. Thanks also go to Patricia Davis-Muffett, Jeanette Gundel, Robert Sanders, and an anonymous reviewer for comments on a prior draft. Earlier versions of this article were presented at the 1993 meetings of the Society for Research in Child Development and the American Association for Applied Linguistics (AAAL).

Correspondence concerning this article should be sent to Amy Sheldon, Department of Speech-Communication, 460 Folwell Hall, University of Minnesota, 9 Pleasant Street, SE, Minneapolis, MN 55455. E-mail: asheldon@maroon.tc.umn.edu process throughout one's lifetime. Much of our thinking about conflict has negative connotations, however. Conflict is often likened to a war-like activity, that is, a disagreement that has the potential to escalate into chaos and destruction. A dictionary definition of *conflict* is the following (Gove et al., 1967):[1]

> 1: a clash, competition, or mutual interference of opposing or incompatible forces, antagonism; 2: an engagement of men under arms: struggle, contest, fight; prolonged fighting, warfare.

A definition that frames conflict primarily as a heavy-handed adversarial activity is hardly gender neutral. Heavy-handed contests (both verbal and physical) fit hegemonic masculine gender stereotypes in many cultures (see Connell, 1987, for discussion of "hegemonic" masculinity) and have been shown to be more typical of Euro-American and Afro-American boys' behavior than of girls' (Maccoby & Jacklin, 1974, 1980; DiPietro, 1981; Miller, Danaher, & Forbes, 1986; Archer, Pearson, & Westeman, 1988; Sheldon, 1990; Leaper, 1991). Goodwin (1980), Sheldon (1992a), and Sheldon and Johnson (1994) pointed out, however, that girls are just as competent as boys in direct and confrontational conflict talk, but stronger social penalties for females engaging in such behavior create an effective deterrent. Nevertheless, there are very effective indirect and less confrontational verbal strategies for conflict management. This article is about such dispute management strategies.

In previous articles I have described a highly assertive feminine conflict style, called "double-voice discourse," which has an overlay of mitigation and has the effect of softening rather than escalating discord (Sheldon, 1992a, 1992b; Sheldon & Johnson, 1994). I have argued that double-voice discourse is a reflection of stricter social constraints on females than males to "say it with a smile" (Sachs, 1987), "be nice," and avoid social discord (see Sheldon, 1992a; Sheldon & Johnson, 1994).

Double-voice discourse as a style of conflict talk is better described by the term *negotiation,* which is defined as follows:

> [from Latin *negotiatus,* past participle of *negotiari* to carry on business] 1. to communicate with another so as to arrive at the settlement of some matter: . . . to arrive through discussion at some kind of agreement or compromise about something; 2. to deal with (some matter or affair that requires ability for its successful handling) . . . . (Gove et al., 1967)

Highly mitigated exchanges such as those in double-voicing have been noticed by others who study girls' discourse (e.g., Miller et al., 1986; Sachs, 1987; Hughes, 1988). Recent research (e.g., Rundquist, 1992; Ely, Gleason, & McCabe, 1996; Reese, Haden, & Fivush, 1996; Gleason, Ely, Perlmann, & Narasimhan, in press) indicates that gender differences in conflict talk among peers have roots in gender-related patterns of parent–child discourse.

There is a belief among researchers that conflict can have important positive outcomes for a child's social, linguistic, and cognitive development (Goodwin, 1980; Goodwin & Goodwin, 1987; Corsaro & Rizzo, 1990; Sheldon, 1990, 1992a; Shantz & Hartup, 1992). However, demonstrations are needed of how children actually use their complex sociolinguistic skills to navigate through social discord.

This article focuses on the discourse skills used by some White, middle-class, advantaged preschool girls to manage their disagreements.[2] I show how their management of opposition is a jointly constructed achievement. As such, it requires the coordination of high levels of sociolinguistic skill to arrive at cooperative as well as self-serving, competitive, or discordant ends. I have chosen to discuss an example of a *sustained* and *discontinuous* opposition for three reasons: (1) sustained conflict can reveal much about the depth and complexity of sociolinguistic skills; (2) it is rarely described in the developmental conflict talk literature; and (3) it is fairly common in preschoolers' interactions, especially during pretend play.[3]

The episode discussed here is an example of social ostracism. Exclusivity has been shown to be a key factor in the organization of older and adolescent girls' groups (e.g., Feshbach & Sones, 1971; Eder & Hallinan, 1978; Daniels-Beirness, 1989; Goodwin, 1990b; Cowan & Underwood, 1995). In a study of gender differences in exclusionary behavior among fourth graders, Cairns and Cairns (1984) found that ignoring occurred most often in girls' conflicts with other girls. From fourth through ninth grades, social ostracism in girls' disputes with other girls greatly increases (Cairns, Cairns, Neckerman, Ferguson, & Gariepy, 1989). Ostracism occurs more often in older girls' than in older boys' disputes, and girls report experiencing ostracism more frequently than boys report it.

The conflict episode discussed here reveals that in connection with their pretend play at least, some preschool girls already are skillful in verbally engineering ostracism. And some have learned how to verbally resist being ostracized by making themselves socially desirable. The behaviors associated with ostracism may even be underreported in younger girls' groups.

PROCEDURE

The example of negotiated opposition analyzed here comes from a larger study of 36 three-, four-, and five-year-old preschoolers. They were videotaped in unsupervised, spontaneous play at their daycare center. Friends were grouped into same-sex triads. The groups were brought into a room on three different occasions where they played for approximately 25 minutes. The room was set up with different gender-preferred resources on each occasion (Lloyd, Duveen, & Smith, 1988): either as a housekeeping center (with girl-preferred resources), a trucks-blocks-dinosaur center (with boy-preferred resources), or as an art center (with gender-neutral resources). The example took place in the group's Trucks session.[4] It was one of several longer negotiations that occurred in girls' groups in the study.[5]

The Conflict Episode: "I'm Really Getting Tired of Waiting"

The episode contains a disagreement between two girls, Tulla and Eva, about whether Tulla can be included in the pretend play that Eva is planning. Eva wants to create a scenario that only includes Kelly, the third girl in the triad. The opposition between Eva and Tulla continues to resurface in between stretches of enacted pretend play. Eva tries to regulate Tulla's involvement and creates justifications, within the pretend frame, for excluding her. But Tulla persists in negotiating a role for herself in the unfolding story. She makes her pretend character relevant to the ongoing action and voices her objections also within the logic of the pretend frame. This conflict, then, is a case study of girls' power struggle over access and inclusion. It describes how Eva and Tulla use the resources of pretend play, manipulating the pretend frame itself by stepping in and out of it, to argue for or against Tulla's relevance and desirability.

Similarity Between Theater and Negotiating Play

There is a likeness between pretend play and theater. The language of pretending embodies both the planning and enactment of a story. There are stagecraft roles as well as character roles to be played. These roles engage a child in imagining, brainstorming, evaluating, and revising the script; creating a set and arranging the props; enacting the script; directing and responding to the enactment; being an onstage player or standing by offstage; being an audience; and so on.

The similarity between the negotiation of pretend play and elements of theater offers a fruitful comparison for discussing this conflict episode.[6] Eva and Kelly are center-stage because Eva regulates the planning and enactment of the story as the principal actor and stage manager (see discussion of the stage manager voice in Wolf & Hicks, 1989). She chooses Kelly as her co-player and keeps Tulla offstage, as a bystander or audience, throughout most of the episode. But Tulla continues to nudge her companions from the edge of their play for an onstage role, offering script suggestions to make her role desirable and timely.

The following analysis describes how Eva's and Tulla's attempts to influence each other, negotiate their differences, and get what they want are linguistically and pragmatically constructed. The girls are extremely skillful in techniques of double-voice discourse that combine self-interest with social savvy. These speakers possess verbal negotiation skills that enable them to confront without being very confrontational; to clarify without backing down; and to use mitigators, indirectness, and even subterfuge to soften the blow while promoting their own wishes. They negotiate with a rich variety of techniques (e.g., justifications, postponements, reframings, token agreements that preface refusals, dramatic imagery, and wonderful leaps of imagination), which elevate conflict above the level of mere rounds of refusal, keep the disagreement from disrupting the social fabric, and allow the "show to go on."

"Pretend We Wanted to Get Married, Right?":
Establishing the Wedding Scenario

Eva (4;9), Kelly (5;5), and Tulla (4;7) have been sitting in a semicircle, playing with large and small dinosaurs, ridable trucks, smaller dump trucks, and shovel trucks. Each one also has a miniature toy person. The sequence that follows starts with Eva suggesting a switch into a pretend frame and a new play theme. Eva's plan includes Kelly but not Tulla.[7]

1	Eva:	((*to no one in particular*)) Pretend you- we- we wanted to get married, right? Pretend we wanted to ⌈get-
2	Kelly:	((*putting dinosaurs in her truck*)) ⌊Who?
3	Tulla:	((*to Eva*)) Yeah, ((*to Kelly*)) us!
4	Eva:	Yeah.
5	Kelly:	((*to Eva*)) Me? My guy?
6	Eva:	((*to Kelly*)) Yeah, we both wanted to get married, ⌈right?
7	Tulla:	((*to Eva*)) ⌊Ho- how
8		'bout mine? ((*"mine" possibly refers to Tulla's toy person*))
9	Kelly:	((*responding to Eva in line 6*)) Right.

This strip of talk is constructed with a variety of double-voice discourse techniques that present the soon-to-be-controversial script in a self-serving but mitigated fashion (see Sheldon, 1992a, 1992b; Sheldon & Johnson, 1994). In line 1, Eva uses a joint directive with "pretend" that is also a tag question which asks for agreement, "Pretend you- we . . . wanted to get married, right?" In lines 2–5, Kelly and Tulla try to clarify which one Eva meant to include, and Tulla thinks the suggestion includes her. In line 6, Eva repeats her joint directive with a tag question, clarifying that her proposal includes Kelly, but specifies no role for Tulla. She repeats her request for confirmation from Kelly, "we both wanted to get married, right?" In line 9, Kelly agrees, whereas in lines 7–8, Tulla requests to be included but mitigates it by framing the request as a suggestion, framing the request indirectly, as a question, "How 'bout mine?"[8]

Negotiating Inclusion in the Marriage Script

As the principal roles of wife and husband are now assigned, the next segment of discourse finds Eva and Tulla discussing how Tulla could—in principle—be included. Eva's alliance with Kelly is solidified by giving Tulla a secondary role. As it will turn out, it will be a rather nonexistent role but one that is consistent with the logic of the emerging domestic script. Meanwhile, Kelly, whose participation is assured, sits nearby taking toys in and out of a truck, but taking little if any part in the girls' discussion.

10	Tulla:	((*to Eva*)) How 'bout MINE? ((*i.e., her toy person*))
11	Eva:	Yeah. No, yours didn't- you have to be the brother,
12		remember?
13	Tulla:	Oh, yeah, I'll be the baby brother. ((*giggles*))
14	Kelly:	((*continues to play with dinosaurs and a truck*))
15	Eva:	((*to Tulla*)) Yeah, you have to be a baby brother.
16	Tulla:	Yeah, I was growing into your tummy.
17	Eva:	Yeah, but not yet.
18	Tulla:	Yeah, but not yet. You didn't eat enough yet, right?
19	Eva:	No. =
20	Kelly:	= No. Cuz pretend- =
21	Eva:	= Pretend we wanted to get married, right?

In line 10, Tulla repeats her wish to be part of the marriage scenario too. But Eva, acting as the stage manager directing their play, does not want her to participate, yet. In lines 11-12, Eva doesn't refuse Tulla outright but postpones her participation instead, consigning Tulla to the ordinarily desirable role of a sibling ("you have to be the brother, remember?").

Justifying One's Actions and Controlling Other's Reactions: "You Have to be the Brother, Remember?"

Throughout the entire episode, Eva and Tulla give plausible justifications to persuade each other to comply with their respective wishes. Their use of justifications in conflict talk is consistent with a gender-based pattern for preschoolers found by Kyratzis (1992, p. 327). She noticed that girls use more justifications than boys and try to "justify the fit of their control move [e.g., directives, plans] to the overall theme or topic . . . in terms of a group goal." Kyratzis claimed that this reflects the relationship orientation in girls' groups. However, it also reveals their orientation to the workings of power and status in their group and how to get it.

The following is an analysis of Eva's statement in lines 11–12, "you have to be the brother, remember?" Eva is reminding Tulla that she proposed to take the role of the brother 148 turns earlier, although they did not have a play script planned at that time.

Eva:	((*to Tulla and Kelly*)) Pretend this one ((*a toy person*)) was my husband, right?
Kelly:	Right.
Tulla: →	And this ((*another toy person*)) is your brother, right? ((*pause*)) Some brothers are big.
Eva:	But he only knows how to drive those kinda ones, right? ((*referring to a truck*))
Tulla:	Yeah, and not real cars.

But with the subsequent emergence of the wedding scenario, Eva wants to play with Kelly, and it is not a good time for Tulla to enter their play. Reintroducing a pretend role that Tulla expressed interest in earlier provides a justification for postponing Tulla's participation now.

The tactic Eva is taking in lines 11–12 is a particularly subtle example of double-voicing. It is a sophisticated use of language to pursue her own agenda without disrupting the social fabric of the group. Eva reintroduces their previous discussion but reshapes it so it is relevant to what she is doing now.

Rather than *ask* Tulla, she presupposes that Tulla wants to, or will, continue in that same role now, when she says in lines 11–12, "you have to be the brother, remember?" *Remember?* is a tag that requests agreement, like *right?* or *ok?* But *remember?* is different than these. It is a factive verb. It presupposes the *truth* of the claim that Tulla had agreed to play the role of brother. Eva also frames Tulla's obligation to the brother role by the way that she constructs the matrix sentence that precedes the tag. It places Tulla in a somewhat difficult position because Eva phrases it as an imperative for Tulla, "you have to be the brother." If Tulla were to contest Eva's demand, it would intensify their conflict. Note that Eva could have described Tulla's participation in a variety of other ways that would entail less obligation and would have made it easier for Tulla to refuse or negotiate than "you have to be." For example, Eva might have said: "how 'bout you be the brother" or "you're the brother" or "you're supposed to be the brother" or even "you said you would be the brother."

Eva's use of the tag *remember?*, rather than *ok?* or *right?*, also makes the process of refusal more complicated for Tulla. For example, Tulla would have to deny or dispute what she said previously or would have to explain that just because she talked earlier about making her toy person be the brother does not obligate her to that role right now. However it might be done, countering Eva's *remember?* seems to involve a more complicated refusal than countering an *ok?* or *right?* would.

"Yes, but" as a Strategy to Preface Refusal With Token Agreement

Eva's "remember?" is effective in getting Tulla to stay in the role of brother even though Tulla wants to be the husband.[9] In line 13, Tulla agrees to be the baby brother. In line 15, Eva begins a "yes, but" move, in which agreement prefaces disagreement, or token willingness prefaces actual refusal (see Pomerantz, 1984; Sacks, 1987; Sheldon, 1992a, 1992b, for other examples of this strategy and discussion of a preference for agreement in conversation). Eva tells Tulla that she can be the baby brother. After Tulla accommodates and adds the constraint that the baby is still growing in Eva's tummy, in line 16, Eva builds the "but" component onto Tulla's turn and adds that the baby brother is not yet growing in her tummy. With these conditions imposed, and without directly refusing Tulla, Eva maneuvers Tulla out of her play. She has defined a potential role for Tulla, but one that is not actualized. Still, the promise is there. Tulla is symbolically included in the story plan, even if her participation is delayed. The result is an ambiguous inclusion of Tulla that is not exactly a refusal. The ambiguity is likely to temper opposition if Tulla were inclined to voice it. In short, Eva's tag question in lines 11-12, coupled with her "yes, but" tactic in lines 15 and 17, captures much cognitive and interactional complexity.

Resisting Ostracism: Seeking to Make Oneself Relevant, Justifying a Place for One's Character in the Script

In the following section, Eva directs her attention to Kelly, and although Tulla asks a number of questions and tries to invent ways to justify her entrance into their play, she is either ignored or admonished

to "be quiet." This further postpones her entry into the play; she is kept
off stage for quite a while.[10]

22	Tulla:	Yeah. And then you were- after you got married you
23		wanted a re-
24	Kelly:	((*puts her toy person in Eva's dump truck*))
25	Eva:	((*to toy person Kelly put in her truck, spoken in a high-*
26		*pitched playful voice*)) WHAT ARE YOU DOING HERE?
27	Tulla:	Yeah. =
28	Kelly:	((*high-pitched voice*)) ⌐MA::::!
29	Tulla:	└PRETEND ONE OF YOU
30		WANTED ⌐A REAL BABY BROTHER.
31	Eva:	((*to Tulla*)└SH:::! BE QUIET! ((*Eva had put her toy person*
32		*on Tulla's truck, and talked to her impatiently, in the high-*
33		*pitched voice of the toy*))
34	Tulla:	((*brings her own toy person up to Eva's and uses a high-*
35		*pitched squeaky voice*)) OKAY, YOU WO- I WON'T BE YOUR
36		BROTHER ANY MORE! ((*Tulla moves her toy person away in*
37		*a huff, turns her back on Eva, and concentrates on playing*
38		*with her own truck and toys*))

Tulla tries to enter the play in line 22 and then again in line 27 with
the justification that now that Eva is married, Tulla's role deserves to be
played. Tulla wants the baby-in-the-tummy to materialize, to become
"real" so she can have something to do ("after you were married you
wanted a re-"). But Eva and Kelly are unconvinced and continue to play,
ignoring Tulla. In lines 29–30, Tulla tries again, loudly repeating an
indirect directive to make herself heard over Kelly, "PRETEND ONE OF
YOU WANTED A REAL BABY BROTHER." In line 31, Eva interrupts Tulla
and admonishes her, in the falsetto of her character's voice, "SH:::!
BE QUIET"! Her words are direct, angry, and confrontational. Tulla
counters angrily in lines 35–36 with a "yes, but" reply, a threat that is
further mitigated because it is still within the pretend frame and is
spoken in the falsetto of her toy person, "OKAY . . . I WON'T BE YOUR BROTHER
ANY MORE!"

Ventriloquating: Animating One's Character
as a Conflict Management Strategy

The girls mark the fact that they are speaking in the pretend frame
by speaking as their toy characters. They speak in the first person, using

a high-pitched falsetto voice. Animating[11] the toy person as a speaker creates an intimacy with the invented character. It also blurs the distinction between oneself, the child, and one's character or role. This takes some of the responsibility away from the child for what she is saying, making it look as if the child is not the author of the words, and that someone outside of the child, the character, is saying the words as part of the story. Animating another's voice implicitly marks a shift in frame to "pretend." As I have discussed elsewhere (Sheldon, 1990), being in the pretend play frame helps to mitigate conflict.

Wolf, Rygh, and Altschuler (1984, p. 212) found gender differences in children's patterns of affiliation with the characters they create. Girls are more likely to "speak through the [toy] figures to create a first person conversational narrative" than boys are.[12] Animating another's voice also gives the girls more freedom to be direct and confrontational than they might feel they had if they were to speak in their "own" words, or in Goffman's (1981) terms, as the "principal."

Angry Words Exchanged in Quiet Tones: A Form of Double-Voice Discourse

When the girls speak as a character in the story, animating a voice other than their own, it can also distance them from the effect of their utterances, which are now direct and confrontational. There is a lack of congruence between their angry words and the squeaky, constructed falsetto in which they are spoken. Sheldon (1992b, pp. 534–535) discussed a similar example of lack of congruence between form and content when girls exchange angry words, yet say them in a whispered, hushed fashion. Related to this, Linell and Bredmar's (1994, p. 14) study of talk between women noted that Swedish midwives changed their voice quality to indicate that they were discussing a delicate topic when talking with pregnant women.

Managing Conflict by Ignoring and Withdrawing

After Tulla turns her back (lines 36–38), Eva and Kelly move closer to one another and continue playing the marriage script together. Tulla begins to narrate her own separate play theme and remains offstage with her back turned to Eva and Kelly. She periodically looks over her shoulder to watch their interaction. This continues until line 60, when Eva asks Tulla a question outside of the pretend frame, which brings her back into the group, if not their play, for a short time.

39 Kelly: ((*puts her miniature toy in Eva's dump truck*))
40 Eva: ((*brings her toy person up to the one Kelly put in*
41   *her truck and speaks irritatedly in the falsetto voice*
42   *of her toy person*)) NOW, WHAT DO YOU WANT?
43 Kelly: ((*moves her toy person closer to Eva's and uses a*
44   *falsetto voice*)) SHOULD WE GET MARRIED?
45 Tulla: ((*Turns from her own play and watches Eva and Kelly*))
46 Eva: ((*falsetto*)) LET ME SEE ABOUT THIS. ((*She moves her*
47   *toy person to her side of the truck away from Kelly's*))
48 Kelly: ((*falsetto*)) ⌈OKAY, YOU GO HOME- ((*takes her toy person*
49   *back to her truck and watches Eva*))
50 Eva: ((*falsetto*)) ⌊FOR MY REAL HUSBAND- FOR MY REAL
51   HUSBAND ((*looking at her toy person*))
52 Eva: ((*to Kelly in her own voice*)) Pretend you were my real
53   husband.
54 Kelly: Right.
55 Tulla: ((*playing by herself, adjacent to Eva and Kelly, gestures*
56   *toward Eva with her dinosaur, says something inaudible in*
57   *a high voice*))
58 Eva: ((*to Kelly, in a high voice*)) You're number B.[13] ((*She*
59   *looks at the letter on her own vest*)) I'm number A. ((*To*
60   *Tulla*)) What number are you, C?

Resisting Ostracism by Bringing One's Character to Life

The three girls get diverted into a discussion about what the letters on their vests mean (omitted here) and then Eva ignores Tulla again and she and Kelly move closer to one another to resume playing with their toy people at Eva's truck. Tulla is sitting near Kelly's side and Kelly turns her back to her. Tulla continues as if standing by, offstage as the audience, ignored. She moves slightly away from them and plays with her own truck for a while. Then she attempts to persuade them again.

77 Tulla: Sh::::! ((*in a falsetto pretend voice*)) ⌈I'M SLEEPING.
78 Kelly: ⌊((*laughs, not*
79   *clear why*))

80	Tulla:	((*excitedly*)) You know who's ⌈sleeping? Your <u>brother's</u> =
81	Kelly:	((*looking up at ceiling*)) ⌊Bright lights.
82	Tulla:	=sleeping. ((*gleefully*)) Hee ee! Lookit, he's sleeping!
83		((*She brings her truck over to Eva and Kelly and points to*
84		*her toy person lying in the shovel of the truck*))
85	Eva:	((*To Tulla*)) He's still in the TUMMY. He's still in the
86		TUMMY.
87	Kelly:	((*She turns and takes the "sleeping" toy person from Tulla's*
88		*truck, lifting it high in the air as if to drop it in her own*
89		*truck*)) ⌈Dum:ps:ter!
90	Tulla:	((*Quietly*)) ⌊Don't. ((*She reaches up and takes her toy back*))

Starting in line 77, Tulla tries to get the girls' attention in a variety of ways without moving out of the pretend frame. She indirectly asks them to stop their play by making a dramatic sound, "Sh:::!" This signals that someone is sleeping. She starts to enact her role as the baby, first as the first person narrator, ""I'M SLEEPING," and then (lines 80 and 82) as the observing narrator, "Your <u>brother's</u> sleeping." She directs Eva's and Kelly's attention to an actual, *embodied* baby brother, represented by a toy figure in her truck. She moves the figure closer to them, points at it, and says, "Lookit, he's sleeping!" (line 82). In this way, she tries to get herself accepted in their play. She actualizes the character of the baby brother. She makes the baby relevant to the ongoing activity. She makes it appealing, but also unobtrusive.

She tries to get the others involved in her script in other ways. She challenges them to guess who the toy in her truck is supposed to be (line 80: "You know who's sleeping?"), almost as a test of shared knowledge. She refers to the baby as a member of their family, someone they are connected to and, by implication, should be interested in or have something to do with ("Your brother's sleeping!"). She brings the baby closer, into their line of sight, and demands that they acknowledge it and, by association, acknowledge and accept her ("Lookit").

Managing Conflict by Postponement Rather Than Direct Refusal: A Double-Voice Strategy

Yet in lines 85–86, Eva is not persuaded. She stays in control of the agenda and, in a double-voice refusal, counters, "He's still in the TUMMY. He's still in the TUMMY." Once again Eva postpones incorporating Tulla into her story, without entirely refusing her either, keeping the baby a possibility not yet realized. Eva continues to play with Kelly.

More Double-Voice Discourse: Angry Words
Exchanged in a Hushed Voice

91	Eva:	((*to Kelly*)) Let's get- pretend we're getting married
92		now, 'kay?
93	Tulla:	And you- ((*Eva and Kelly are humming the Wedding March,*
94		*ignoring Tulla*)) one of you- Eva? Eva:? Eva! Eva! Eva!
95		Pretend- preten-
96	Eva:	((*to Tulla*)) Uh-uh! I'm talking to her. ((*Eva and Kelly face*
97		*Tulla*))
98	Tulla:	Can I tell you something after?
99	Eva:	Sure. ((*glares at Tulla and impatiently hisses*)) Just be quiet!
100	Tulla:	'Kay, I been trying to be.
101	Eva:	((*to Kelly as she enacts a wedding with their two toy people*))
102		Okay, 'kay, do you deserve to get married? Yes. Do you
103		deserve to love each other? Yes. ((*giggles*))
104	Tulla:	⌜I ge- I'm uh, really getting tired of waiting.
105	Eva:	⌞Do you deserve- do you deserve to love each other?
106		Yes. You may kiss ((*makes two toys "kiss"; she and*
107		*Kelly giggle, ignoring Tulla*))

In lines 91–92, after Eva suggests to Kelly "Let's . . . pretend we're getting married now" the two girls move toward one another and again turn their backs to Tulla. They stay this way as they hum the Wedding March. Tulla continually tries to get Eva's attention in line 94, at one point tapping her on the shoulder and speaking outside of the pretend frame. Eva finally acknowledges Tulla brusquely in line 96. But she admonishes her in line 99 in a "yes, but" move in which token agreement, "Sure," prefaces a hissed, direct refusal, "Just be quiet?"[14] Even though the opposition escalates in line 99, verbally and nonverbally, Eva's speaking voice is muted. In line 100, Tulla replies that she's been trying to accommodate Eva. In lines 101–103, Eva returns to the wedding script, narrating the voices of all the participants, as Tulla and Kelly look on.

Resisting Ostracism: Complaining
and Being Ignored

In line 104, Tulla interjects a complaint about waiting so long. The others ignore her. Then Tulla steps outside of the pretend frame and suggests a relevant new subtheme.

108	Tulla:	It's not funny. I need a question now. Pretend one of
109		you wanted a baby really much then- ⌈that you had =
110	Kelly:	((*to Eva in the wedding, falsetto*)) ⌊Oᴋᴀʏ.
111	Tulla:	= to get ⌈one
112		⌊((*Eva and Kelly hum the Wedding March, as Eva*
113		*moves her and Kelly's toy people along the floor*))
114	Tulla:	You got a baby in the 'doptive place.
115	Eva:	((*To Tulla*)) Yeah, but I didn't go yet. =
116		((*To Kelly, referring to their toy people*)) = Now,
117		we're dancing, right? ⌈((*hums dancing music*))
118	Tulla:	⌊Yeah, and then you wan⌈ted one.
119	Kelly:	((*To Eva, still humming*)) ⌊I'll hold
120		this one.

Tulla's suggestion in lines 108–109 and 111 is ignored. Eva and Kelly continue their play. Kelly interrupts Tulla in line 110, and in line 112, she and Eva break into Tulla's complaint, humming the Wedding March while walking their toy figures down an imaginary aisle and making them kiss. Tulla tries to develop the narrative again in line 114, "You got a baby in the 'doptive place." This gets another "yes, but" refusal from Eva in line 115, "Yeah, but I didn't go yet," followed by a narration in lines 116–117 and 119–120 of Eva's and Kelly's continued activity in the pretend frame, "Now we're dancing, right?" Tulla persists in line 118, still outside of the pretend frame, with a "yes, but" tactic of her own that offers a justification framed in terms of Eva's interests—that after the marriage Eva will be ready for a baby. Tulla is still ignored though and remains a bystander while half-heartedly playing with her truck, off-stage. There is then a diversion from the script as the three girls talk, animating their pretend characters' voices, about who has long or short hair and which length they prefer. Then play continues.

Success at Last

128	Eva:	((*to Kelly, falsetto*)) Yᴏᴜ ɢᴏ ɢᴇᴛ ʏᴏᴜʀ ᴛʀᴜᴄᴋ.
129	Kelly:	((*falsetto*)) Oᴋᴀʏ. Wʜᴇʀᴇ sʜᴏᴜʟᴅ I ᴍᴇᴇᴛ ʏᴏᴜ?
130	Eva:	((*ғᴀʟsᴇᴛᴛᴏ*)) Uᴍ ᴀᴛ- ᴀᴛ ᴍᴀʀᴋᴇᴛ- ᴛʜᴇ ᴍᴀʀᴋᴇᴛ- ᴛʜᴇ
131		ᴍᴀʀᴋᴇᴛᴘʟᴀᴄᴇ.
132	Tulla:	((*falsetto, distressed voice of baby brother*)) Oʜ ɴᴏ!
133	Kelly:	((*falsetto, to Eva*)) ⌈Wʜɪᴄʜ ᴍᴀʀᴋᴇᴛ?
134	Tulla:	⌊Nᴏᴛ ᴀɢᴀɪɴ! I'ᴠᴇ ᴡᴀɪᴛᴇᴅ sᴏ ʟᴏɴɢ.
135		Gᴏᴅ!
136	Eva:	((*To Tulla*)) You're still in my tummy, ʀɪɢʜᴛ? =

137	Tulla:	=No, no, at the 'doptive place.
138	Eva:	Nobody adopt you yet, right? =
139	Kelly:	((*falsetto, to Eva*)) ⌈OKAY ((*playing with her truck*))
140	Tulla:	((*to Eva*)) ⌊=Yeah. ((*louder, talking over*
141		*Kelly*)) Because there was only one, one baby, right? =
142	Eva:	((*to Tulla*)) =left, ⌈right? =
143	Kelly:	((*falsetto*)) ⌊OKAY ⌈LADIES. ⌈OKAY.
144	Tulla:	⌊=Yeh. ((*louder*)) ⌊ And then
145		people were about ⌈to-
146	Eva:	((*falsetto*)) ⌊OH, I THINK WE SHOULD GO TO THE
147		DOCTOR'S AND GET OUR BABY. =
148	Kelly:	((*falsetto*)) =OKAY. ((*Kelly and Eva make vehicle noises*
149		*and push their trucks over to Tulla's truck*))
⋮		
151	Tulla:	((*puts her toy person in the shovel of her truck, opens the*
152		*shovel and drops the toy person out, and says gleefully,*
153		*falsetto*)) THERE'S YOUR BABY!!

The wedding is completed prior to line 128 and in the subsequent lines new decisions are made about the script. In lines 132, 134–135, Tulla speaks in the falsetto voice of her toy figure once again to express her exasperation at still being put off. Animating her character's voice allows her to mitigate the impatience, disappointment, and confrontation she expresses directly and in the first person, "OH NO! NOT AGAIN! I'VE WAITED SO LONG. GOD!" Eva finally takes notice and they collaborate on a script that includes Tulla. Moving seamlessly out of the pretend frame, in line 136 Eva asks Tulla for clarification of the story line, "You're still in my tummy, right?" Tulla counters that she's at the " 'doptive place." Eva then gives a reason why "the baby" is available for adoption, which Tulla elaborates on. In lines 146–147, Eva finally brings Tulla into the story when her character declares to Kelly in a mitigated joint directive, "OH, I THINK WE SHOULD GO TO THE DOCTOR'S AND GET OUR BABY." Kelly's character agrees, and in line 153 Tulla gleefully brings the baby onstage and incorporates it into the girls' play.

CONCLUSION

Negotiating for Symbolic Interpersonal Goods

This long conflict episode arises from a frequent and challenging event in childhood: entering into the play of one's peers. Entering play and coordinating with others calls on a variety of social, linguistic, and cognitive skills. Collaborative play also poses the challenge of competing with others for power and status as well as negotiating with them to achieve consensus and reciprocity. The episode discussed in this article is an extended negotiation for these symbolic goods. The analysis of talk demonstrates these children's sociolinguistic competence.

Tulla tries a variety of ways to justify her inclusion and to persuade Eva, who is blocking access. The negotiation is maintained for a long time even though it is interrupted by some side discussions. Eva keeps Tulla from actively participating but Tulla becomes impatient with her exclusion and does not allow herself to be put off indefinitely. She persists in offering Eva relevant ways to include her and acts as if she expects Eva to comply. In asking for social reciprocity she is also asking for fairness. There is a moral dimension to this opposition, and Tulla holds Eva accountable.[15] Eva, having planned and enacted a certain order of events in a domestic script, finally allows Tulla to incorporate her role, which had been postponed so long.[16]

The Episode as a Unit of Analysis

Close sequential analysis of complex discourse episodes like this one offers a number of advantages in the study of children's social uses of language. Various double-voice discourse strategies that occurred in an utterance or a turn were discussed, but the full episode that contains them is also considered. Keeping track of the entire episode reveals ways in which single utterances are contingent on the context and how they are threads of an interconnected text. The entire episode affects the meaning of the individual utterances; therefore, the whole episode must be retained as a unit of analysis.

Keeping the whole episode in view also gives a sense of how *the children* track the discourse through this long and involved opposition. And it shows how the pretend and nonpretend play frames shift and are interwoven through the opposition. The pretend frame begins as the context in which the opposition between the girls arises. It is subsequently recruited by each of them as a symbolic resource to manage the opposition: to mitigate, postpone, and finally resolve that opposition.

Discussing the varieties of double-voice discourse in the context of the entire episode shows that the girls choose linguistic and pragmatic strategies that are contingently relevant to preceding talk and events.

Their mitigated talk must be sensitive to the play situation, as well as to what their companions have said and might say, in order to be effective.

Clearly, conflict can be an extremely complex verbal and social interactional "achievement" (see Putallaz & Sheppard, 1992). In light of this, our understanding of such complex social behaviors should not be based only on the study of shorter and simpler turn exchanges, or only on the extraction of aggregated patterns, which are discussed outside of the context that produced them. This will underrepresent the complexity of the speakers' understanding of language and social interaction and their use of language to accomplish social goals (for further discussion of the promise and challenge provided by a focus on discourse analysis of local cultures in studies of child development see, e.g., Eckert & McConnell-Ginet, 1992; Dunn, 1992; Garvey, 1992; and Schegloff, 1993).

This episode is also an illustration of the paradox of conflictual interaction. Oppositional behavior is highly coordinated and involves cooperative activities too. In addition, the opposition displays how children creatively draw on a variety of resources—knowledge of the world; linguistic, pragmatic, social, imaginative, and moral competences—to achieve their own goals, as well as shared ends. The use of double-voice discourse to manage conflict allows them to soften and even mask disagreement (e.g., the "yes, but" strategy). This in turn avoids disruption and allows a high level of collaborative imaginative play to emerge.

Discourse Analysis as a Tool for Testing
Gender Stereotypes

The episode discussed here also contradicts the stereotype that girls are not effective at verbally managing conflict, or that they lack a competitive dynamic (e.g., Miller et al., 1986). Rather, this example, like others encountered in this community of children (Sheldon, 1990, 1992a, 1993; Sheldon & Johnson, 1994) and elsewhere (Goodwin, 1980, 1987), shows the workings of a peer culture in which young girls are extremely skillful in managing conflict. Discourse examples like this one show how much we still have to learn about the complex sociolinguistic skills with which girls navigate rough social waters: resisting and opposing one another to further their own wishes, negotiating a desirable social self, and engaging with others in elaborative, personally meaningful, *and* mutually coordinated endeavors.

Close analysis of discourse is an essential tool to use in partnership with the construction of feminist theory. Discourse analysis reveals how gender is constructed by intricate but mundane everyday practices, even in the lives of young children. It is hoped that work such as this will bring the study of child language closer to the center of feminist theory making.

NOTES

1 In their study of young children's play, Eisenberg and Garvey (1981, p. 150) defined conflict as "an interaction which grows out of an opposition to a request for action, an assertion, or an action . . . and ends with a resolution or dissipation of conflict."

2 These skills can also be understood as "face-work" (see Brown & Levinson, 1987, pp. 61ff, for a discussion of "face" and politeness). I do not pursue this line of discussion here though.

3 See Sheldon (1990, 1992a, 1992b) for discussions of the interrelatedness between conflict and the pretend play frame.

4 Further details of the procedures used in this study can be found in Sheldon (1990).

5 Sheldon (1990, 1992b) and Sheldon and Johnson (1994) discussed other examples of long negotiations. Long and discontinuous conflict in children's interactions can be overlooked by coding conventions that focus on adjacent turns of talk. Eisenberg and Garvey (1981) found that 92% of conflict episodes in a study of nearly 200 children were less than 10 turns and 66% were shorter than 5. The conflict discussed here was sustained for nearly one hundred turns. This might be largely due to the mitigating techniques used and the fact that it was problematized primarily in the pretend frame. The length of the opposition also reflects the degree of verbal mediation. A variety of problem-solving strategies are used that combine an awareness of the coparticipant's needs with the speaker's attempts to achieve her own ends.

6 Sawyer (1994) independently made a similar point; he analyzed pretend play as a form of improvisational theater.

7 The transcripts use conversation analytic notation developed by Gail Jefferson and described in Atkinson and Heritage (1984).

8   For a discussion of how sex/gender influences the kinds of stories that children in this study create in their social play, see Sheldon and Rohleder (in press).

9   "Remember?" is used only one other time (in the more than 13 hours of conversation recorded in this study) in a similar way in a dispute in another girls' group (discussed in Sheldon, 1992b, p. 532). In that case, it results in partial agreement. Both examples of such strategic choices of tag questions provide counterevidence to the well-known claim that the use of tag questions necessarily indicates powerlessness (e.g., Lakoff, 1973; O'Barr & Atkins, 1980).

10 Text in small capitals in special font marks when the child animates her character's voice. It has the added advantage of clearly signaling when they are acting in the pretend play frame.

11 "Animator" is one of a variety of participation roles that Goffman (1981) identified in his study of adult conversation. Levinson (1988) discussed speaker participation roles and Goffman's work further. These concepts can be applied to children's conversations also. For example, Goodwin (1990a, p. 345) demonstrated the importance of "distinguishing between a *principal* responsible for a statement and the *animator* who quotes that talk" in the analysis of storytelling practices of older children.

12 Wolf et al. (1984) indicated that boys usually adopt a more distant type of affiliation with toy figures and are "more likely to speak about their characters from the vantage point of an observing narrator" than to speak as if they were the characters themselves. In a study of gender differences in adult stories, Johnstone (1993, p. 73) reported that monologic stories told by a group of adult, White, midwestern women contain more constructed dialogue than stories told by males. She interpreted this use of language as creating a world in which linguistic interaction is especially valued by women.

13 The children are each hearing a vest with the letter "A," "B," or "C" on it. The vest was used to identify the child and it has a small microphone clipped to the lapel.

14 Another example of this double-voice strategy of muting one's voice when the opposition becomes very confrontational is found in Sheldon (1992b, p. 534).

15 For an interesting and related discussion of moral accountability in talk about sensitive topics, see Linell and Bredmar (1994).

16 One can only speculate about why this conflict episode is so long and elaborate. If the girls were in their larger preschool group and had other playmate choices, perhaps Tulla would not have tried so hard to enter these particular girls' play, or Eva would not have have hedged her refusals, and so forth. In such circumstances, the entry attempt, and hence the mutual opposition, might have been shorter or more confrontational. It seems, however, that negotiating oppositions in the pretend frame allows for longer and more elaborately developed negotiations, and perhaps more negotiation overall. This is because the pretend frame seems to offer more resources for inventing persuasive justifications and reframings than conflicts in a nonpretend frame. The pretend frame might also encourage more mitigated oppositions because there is another focus that is valued and needs to be maintained—the play itself.

REFERENCES

Archer, J., Pearson, N. A., & Westeman, K. E. (1988). Aggressive behavior of children aged 6–11: Gender differences and their magnitude. *British Journal of Social Psychology, 27,* 371–384.

Atkinson, J. M., & Heritage, J. (Eds.). (1984). *Structures of social action.* Cambridge, England: Cambridge University Press.

Brown, P., & Levinson, S. (1987). *Politeness. Some universals of language usage.* Cambridge, England: Cambridge University Press.

Cairns, R. B., & Cairns, B. D. (1984). Predicting aggressive patterns in girls and boys: A developmental study. *Aggressive Behavior, 10,* 227–242.

Cairns, R. B., Cairns, B. D., Neckerman, N. J., Ferguson, L. L., & Gariepy, J. (1989). Growth and aggression: 1. Childhood to early adolescence. *Developmental Psychology, 25,* 320–330.

Connell, R. W. (1987). *Gender and power.* Stanford, CA: Stanford University Press.

Corsaro, W., & Rizzo, T. (1990). Disputes in the peer culture of American and Italian nursery school children. In A. Grimshaw (Ed.), *Conflict talk* (pp. 21–65). Cambridge, England: Cambridge University Press.

Cowan, B. R., & Underwood, M. (1995). *Sugar and spice and everything nice? A developmental investigation of social aggression among girls.* Ms., Reed College, Portland, OR.

Daniels-Beirness, T. (1989). Measuring peer status in boys and girls: A problem of apples and oranges? In B. H. Schneider et al. (Eds.), *Social competence in developmental perspective* (pp. 107–120). Dordrecht, The Netherlands: Kluwer Academic.

DiPietro, J. A. (1981). Rough and tumble play: A function of gender. *Developmental Psychology, 17,* 50–58.

Dunn, J. (1992). Lessons from the study of children's conversations: A discussion of the *Quarterly* special issue on talk. *Merrill-Palmer Quarterly, 38,* 139–149.

Eckert, P., & McConnell-Ginet, S. (1992). Think practically and look locally: Language and gender as community-based practice. *Annual Review of Anthropology, 21,* 461–490.

Eder, D., & Hallinan, M. T. (1978). Sex differences in children's friendships. *American Sociological Review, 43,* 237–250.

Eisenberg, A. R., & Garvey, C. (1981). Children's use of verbal strategies in resolving conflicts. *Discourse Processes, 4,* 149–170.

Ely, R., Gleason, J. B., & McCabe, A. (1996). "Why didn't you talk to your mommy, honey?" Parents' and children's talk about talk. *Research on Language and Social Interaction, 29,* 7–25.

Feshbach, N., & Sones, G. (1971). Sex differences in adolescent reactions toward newcomers. *Developmental Psychology, 4,* 381–386.

Garvey, C. (1992). Introduction to the special issue on talk and the study of socialization and development. *Merrill-Palmer Quarterly, 38,* iii–viii.

Gleason, J. B., Ely, R., Perlmann, R. Y., & Narasimhan, B. (in press). Patterns of prohibitions in parent–child discourse. In D. I. Slobin, J. Gerhardt, A. Kyratzis, & J. Guo (Eds.), *Social interaction, social context, and language: Essays in honor of Susan Ervin-Tripp.* Mahwah, NJ: Lawrence Erlbaum Associates, Inc.

Goffman, E. (1981). Footing. In *Forms of talk* (pp. 124–159). Philadelphia: University of Pennsylvania Press.

Goodwin, M. H. (1980). Directive-response speech sequences in girls' and boys' task activities. In S. McConnell-Ginet, R. Borker, & N. Furman (Eds.), *Women and language in literature and society* (pp. 157–173). New York: Praeger.

Goodwin, M. H. (1990a). *He-said-she-said: Talk as social organization among Black children.* Bloomington: Indiana University Press.

Goodwin, M. H. (1990b). Tactical uses of stories: Participation frameworks within girls' and boys' disputes. *Discourse Processes, 13,* 33–71.

Goodwin, M. H., & Goodwin, C. (1987). Children's arguing. In S. U. Philips, S. Steele, & C. Tanz (Eds.), *Language, gender and sex in comparative perspective* (pp. 200–248). Cambridge, England: Cambridge University Press.

Gove, P. B. et al. (Eds.). (1967). *Webster's third new international dictionary of the English language.* Springfield, MA: G. & C. Merriam.

Hughes, L. (1988). But that's not *really* mean: Competing in a cooperative mode. *Sex Roles, 19,* 669–687.

Johnstone, B. (1993). Community and contest: Midwestern men and women creating their worlds in conversational storytelling. In D. Tannen (Ed.), *Gender and conversational interaction* (pp. 62–80). Oxford, England: Oxford University Press.

Kyratzis, A. (1992). Gender differences in the use of persuasive justifications in children's pretend play. In K. Hall, M. Bucholtz, & B. Moonwomon (Eds.), *Locating power. Proceedings of the Second Berkeley Women and Language Conference, 2* (pp. 326–337). Berkeley: University of California, Berkeley Linguistic Society.

Lakoff, R. (1973). Language and women's place. *Language in Society, 2,* 45–80.

Leaper, C. (1991). Influence and involvement in children's discourse: Age, gender and partner effects. *Child Development, 62,* 797–811.

Levinson, S. (1988). Putting linguistics on a proper footing. In P. Drew & A. Wootton (Eds.), *Erving Goffman: Exploring the interaction order* (pp. 161–227). Boston: Northeastern University Press.

Linell, P., & Bredmar, M. (1994, April). *Reconstructing topical sensitivity: Aspects of face-work in midwife-pregnant woman talk.* Paper read at the 1994 American Association for Applied Linguistics Conference, Baltimore.

Lloyd, B., Duveen, G., & Smith, C. (1988). Social representations of gender and young children's play: A replication. *British Journal of Developmental Psychology, 6,* 83–88.

Maccoby, E., & Jacklin, C. (1974). *The psychology of sex differences*. Stanford, CA: Stanford University Press.

Maccoby, E., & Jacklin, C. (1980). Sex differences in aggression: A rejoinder and reprise. *Child Development, 51,* 964–980.

Miller, P., Danaher, D., & Forbes, D. (1986). Sex-related strategies for coping with interpersonal conflict in children aged five and seven. *Developmental Psychology, 22,* 543–548.

O'Barr, W. M., & Atkins, B. K. (1980). "Women's language" or "powerless language"? In S. McConnell-Ginet, R. Borker, & N. Furman (Eds.), *Women and language in literature and society* (pp. 79–92). New York: Praeger.

Pomerantz, A. (1984). Agreeing and disagreeing with assessments: Some features of preferred/dispreferred turn shapes. In J. M. Atkinson & J. Heritage (Eds.), *Structures of social action: Studies in conversation analysis* (pp. 57–101). Cambridge, England: Cambridge University Press.

Putallaz, M., & Sheppard, B. (1992). Conflict management and social competence. In C. U. Shantz & W. W. Hartup (Eds.), *Conflict in child and adolescent development* (pp. 330–355). Cambridge, England: Cambridge University Press.

Reese, E., Haden, C., & Fivush, R. (1996). Mothers, fathers, daughters, sons: Gender differences in autobiographical reminiscing. *Research on Language and Social Interaction, 29,* 27–56.

Rundquist, S. (1992). Indirectness: A gender study of flouting Grice's maxims. *Journal of Pragmatics, 18,* 431–449.

Sachs, J. (1987). Preschool boys' and girls' language use in pretend play. In S. U. Philips, S. Steele, & C. Tanz (Eds.), *Language, gender and sex in comparative perspective* (pp. 178–188). Cambridge, England: Cambridge University Press.

Sacks, H. (1987). On the preferences for agreement and contiguity in sequences in conversation. In G. Button & J. R. E. Lee (Eds.), *Talk and social organisation* (pp. 54–69). Clevedon, England: Multilingual Matters.

Sawyer, R. K. (1994). Prepublication book summary of *Pretend play as improvisation: Conversation in the preschool classroom*. Hillsdale, NJ: Lawrence Erlbaum Associates, Inc.

Schegloff, E. (1993). Reflections on quantification in the study of conversation. *Research on Language and Social Interaction, 26,* 99–128.

Shantz, C. U., & Hartup, W. W. (Eds.). (1992). *Conflict in child and adolescent development*. Cambridge, England: Cambridge University Press.

Sheldon, A. (1990). Pickle fights: Gendered talk in preschool disputes. *Discourse Processes, 13,* 5–31.

Sheldon, A. (1992a). Conflict talk: Sociolinguistic challenges to self-assertion and how young girls meet them. *Merrill-Palmer Quarterly, 38,* 95–117.

Sheldon, A. (1992b). Preschool girls' discourse competence: Managing conflict. In K. Hall, M. Bucholtz, & B. Moonwomon (Eds.), *Locating power. Proceedings of the Second Berkeley Women and Language Conference, 2* (pp. 529–539). Berkeley: University of California, Berkeley Linguistic Society.

Sheldon, A., & Johnson, D. (1994). Preschool negotiators: Gender differences in double-voice discourse as a conflict talk style in early childhood. In B. Sheppard, R. Lewicki, & R. Bies (Eds.), *Research on negotiation in organizations: 4* (pp. 27–57). Greenwich, CT: JAI.

Sheldon, A., & Rohleder, L. (in press). Sharing the same world, telling different stories: Gender differences in co-constructed pretend narratives. In D. Slobin, J. Gerhardt, A. Kyratzis, & J. Guo (Eds.), *Social interaction, social context, and language: Essays in honor of Susan Ervin-Tripp*. Mahwah, NJ: Lawrence Erlbaum Associates, Inc.

Wolf, D. P., & Hicks, D. (1989). The voices within narratives: The development of intertextuality in young children's stories. *Discourse Processes, 12,* 329–351.

Wolf, D. P., Rygh, J., & Altschuler, J. (1984). Agency and experience: Actions and states in play narratives. In I. Bretherton (Ed.), *Symbolic play: The development of social understanding* (pp. 195–217). New York: Academic.

Research on Language and Social Interaction, 29(1), 81–96

Gender and Mitigation in 4-Year-Olds' Pretend Play Talk With Siblings

Ganie B. DeHart
Department of Psychology
State University of New York at Geneseo

Recent research offers ample evidence of the existence of gender-distinctive linguistic interaction patterns in preschoolers' peer relationships. By age 5, girls' discourse with peers has consistently been characterized as collaborative and mitigated, whereas boys' peer discourse has been characterized as controlling and unmitigated (Austin, Salehi, & Leffler, 1987; Black & Hazen, 1990; Sheldon, 1990; Leaper, 1991). It has been suggested that interaction with same-sex peers provides a context in which these distinctive interaction styles emerge and are strengthened (Maccoby, 1990). However, it is not known to what extent the gender-distinctive discourse patterns that have been observed are specific to peer relationships and their particular social demands and interaction contexts. We do not know, for example,

Collection of the data used in this study was supported by a University of Minnesota Dissertation Fellowship and the Anderson Fund of the Institute of Child Development, University of Minnesota. I gratefully acknowledge the assistance of Nancy Bemel and Roxane Gudeman in data collection and of Buffy Smith in reliability coding.

Correspondence concerning this article should be sent to Ganie DeHart, Department of Psychology, SUNY at Geneseo, 1 College Circle, Geneseo, NY 14454–1401.

whether similar patterns are present in interactions between preschool-aged siblings.

Sibling relationships are a potentially significant setting for studying the development and use of gender-distinctive linguistic interaction patterns. Dunn (1988) suggested that early sibling relationships are an important context for the development of general social understanding. It is plausible that sibling relationships might also be a useful setting for the development of more specific socially constructed concepts, such as gender-distinctive behavior.

Maccoby (1990) argued that gender differences appear as a function of interactions within specific relationships with others of the same and opposite genders, not as cross-situational individual traits. Various researchers have suggested that gender-distinctive behavior is highly context-dependent and situationally specific (Thorne, 1986; Sheldon, 1990). However, virtually all of the existing research on gender differences in preschoolers' language use has been based on playroom interactions of same-sex dyads or groups. Research that extends the range of interaction partners and interaction contexts is needed for a full description of how preschoolers develop and use gender-distinctive language.

Preschool sibling relationships are an interesting context in which to examine the emergence of gender-distinctive behavior because they offer opportunities for both same-sex and mixed-sex interaction with highly familiar partners. In families with all boys or all girls, children have opportunities for learning, practicing, and perhaps intensifying the interaction patterns typical of their own gender. In families with both boys and girls, children can gain early exposure to and experience dealing with interaction strategies typical of the opposite gender. Indeed, there is some evidence that children with opposite-sex siblings show less intense gender typing than children with same-sex siblings (Brim, 1958; Stoneman, Brody, & MacKinnon, 1986).

Preschool peer relationships also offer opportunities for both same- and mixed-sex interaction, but as early as age 3 children begin to show a preference for playmates of their own gender (Maccoby & Jacklin, 1987). As a result, it is much easier and more common for researchers interested in preschool children's social and linguistic interactions to study same-sex peer interactions, especially in settings in which children are free to choose their own interaction partners. Studies of mixed-sex peer interaction often involve experimenter-created groupings of un-familiar peers.

The present study examines the use of gender-distinctive language in preschool sibling conversations, focusing on mitigation in directives and related forms used during pretend play. Past research on language use in peer pretend play (Sachs, 1987) has found a tendency for girls to show a preference for mitigated forms and boys to show a preference for unmitigated forms. Patterns of mitigation may be different in sibling interaction than in peer interaction, however, because of the differences between the two types of relationships.

Sibling relationships differ from peer relationships along several dimensions that are significant in understanding relationships and their role in children's development (Hinde, 1979; Dunn & Kendrick, 1982; DeHart et al., 1994). Sibling relationships are less symmetrical than most peer relationships, though they are more symmetrical than parent–child relationships. Except in the case of twins, one sibling is always older than the other and therefore more advanced developmen-tally, more experienced at many of the activities siblings engage in together, and generally more powerful and able to dominate in sibling interaction. Preschool sibling relationships are also more intimate than most preschool peer relationships, in the sense of both familiarity and emotional closeness; siblings know more about each other than they know about most peers, and they are likely to find each other's behavior highly predictable. Preschool sibling relationships are more affectively intense but also more affectively mixed than most peer relationships; they often combine strong feelings of affection with equally strong feelings of hostility and envy. Finally, the social demands of sibling relationships are quite different from those of peer relationships. The permanence of the sibling relationship is usually not in question; the likelihood that a particular peer relationship will succeed and continue is uncertain. Maintaining interaction, strengthening friendship bonds, and appearing socially acceptable and likable are high priorities in most positive peer interactions; in sibling interactions, children are generally not concerned with these issues — except in some cases to attempt to do the opposite by avoiding interaction or being intentionally obnoxious to a sister or brother.

All of these differences have potential implications for the role of gender in sibling linguistic interaction, particularly for the use of mitigation. As Tannen (1993) pointed out, issues of power and solidarity are often assumed to underlie many of the differences that have been observed in men's and women's use of language; however, what is often overlooked is that power and solidarity can be defined, expressed, and related to each other in a number of different ways. For example, the pursuit of power and the pursuit of solidarity need not be mutually exclusive. Sheldon (1990, 1992) demonstrated that preschool girls often pursue both simultaneously in their management of conflict with peers.

In sibling relationships, power and solidarity are represented differently than they are in peer relationships. In peer relationships (positive ones, at any rate), the partners generally have fairly equal amounts of power, and both solidarity and the desire to increase and maintain it are assumed to be high. In sibling relationships, however, power is unevenly distributed, and issues of solidarity are murkier. On the one hand, sibling solidarity can sometimes be high — in the context of conflict with parents, for example. On the other hand, children's desire to differentiate themselves from their siblings can also be high, and the desire to increase and maintain solidarity is likely to be much lower than it is with attractive peers.

The uneven power distribution in sibling relationships can affect the use of mitigation in several different ways. Younger siblings might be expected to use mitigated forms in dealing with their more powerful older sisters and brothers, whereas older siblings might be expected to express their superior power by using unmitigated forms. However, older siblings might also use mitigated forms as a tool of persuasion or to soften their attempts to control their younger sisters and brothers, in much the same way that middle-class parents use such forms as question directives rather than imperatives when talking to their young children (Hoff-Ginsberg, 1991).

If gender-distinctive behavior is situation- and partner-specific, there is no particular reason to expect that patterns of mitigation in language use would carry over from peer to sibling interactions. The power imbalance and relative lack of constraints against conflict and abrasiveness in sibling relationships create a very different social context for linguistic interaction than the one found in peer relationships. The demand for mitigated linguistic forms would seem to be much lower in sibling than in peer relationships; the question is whether girls and boys will respond differently to that demand and produce different patterns of mitigated and unmitigated forms in interaction with their siblings.

METHOD

Subjects

Subjects were 32 White, middle-class children, 16 girls and 16 boys, ranging in age from 53 to 62 months, $M = 56.7$ months. Half of the children had a sibling who was approximately 2 years older (age range 76 to 86 months, $M = 81.75$ months), and half had a sibling approximately 2 years younger (age range 30 to 34 months, $M = 31.63$ months). At each age level, the sibling pairs were evenly distributed across the four possible gender compositions (two boys, two girls, older boy and younger girl, older girl and younger boy).

Procedure

As part of a larger study of sibling linguistic interaction (DeHart, 1990), each pair was audiotaped at home for 30 minutes in a semistructured play situation, with an observer keeping detailed context notes on their behavior and other events in the environment. Each sibling pair played with two sets of miniature toys (randomly chosen from a farm set, a village set, a train set, and a canal set) for 15 minutes each, with a short break in between. During one 15-minute period, the older sibling was asked to teach the younger sibling how the toy operated; during the other 15-minute period, the children were simply given the toy and asked to play with it together.

Although the intent of the teaching segment was to encourage asymmetrical social interaction, the children's behavior during the two segments did not differ appreciably. Most older siblings provided a brief demonstration of the toy, after which the children quickly reverted to more typical play (DeHart, 1990). As there were no significant differences between the two segments in amount or type of linguistic interaction, data from both were combined in the present analysis.

Transcription and Coding

The audiotapes of the play sessions were later transcribed, and the context notes taken during the sessions were added to the transcripts.

Pretend play utterances were then identified for further analysis. Pretend play was defined as play in which the child transformed an object, another person, or her/himself into something beyond the present situation. Pretend play utterances included utterances setting up pretend situations ("Let's say this is our cabin at the lake"; "I'll be the mom"), utterances narrating pretend scenarios ("I'm having the duck swim backwards"; "They're going to school now"), and utterances produced in character ("Help! I'm drowning!"). Pretend play utterances had to reflect a nonliteral transformation of an object or a person; thus, utterances involving the dividing up of objects without any nonliteral reference to them (e.g., "I get these blocks, and you can have those") did not count as pretend play utterances.

Pretend play utterances were next classified as *obliges* or *non-obliges,* using categories based on those used by Sachs (1987). These categories were used to allow direct comparisons between the results of this study and those of Sachs's study of gender differences in language use during peer pretend play. An oblige is any utterance that requires a verbal or behavioral response from the listener, including both nonrhetorical questions and directives (Blank & Franklin, 1980).

The coding scheme used by Sachs included 10 specific types of obliges, each of which is classified as *unmitigated, mitigated,* or *other.* The coding scheme used in the present study included these 10 types, plus one more, Permission Questions. Table 1 lists and gives examples of each type of oblige. *Unmitigated obliges* include imperatives, prohibitions, and declarative directives. All three of these forms represent direct, often abrupt attempts to influence a partner's behavior, with little concern for politeness or softening of the request. *Mitigated obliges* include question directives, tag questions, joint directives, pretend directives, state questions, and permission questions. All of these forms request action or information from a partner, but in a milder and more indirect way than the unmitigated forms. Pretend directives are considered mitigated because they express some distancing from normal reality and may function as an indirect way of controlling a partner's behavior or dividing up toys or props. *Other* obliges include informational questions and attentional devices; these forms require a response from the partner, but do not easily fit the mitigated/ unmitigated dichotomy.

All of the utterances identified as obliges were assigned to one of the categories listed in Table 1. In the few cases in which an utterance fit

TABLE 1
Categories and Examples of Obliges

Unmitigated obliges	
Imperatives	*Give me the duck.*
Prohibitions	*Don't touch the duck.*
Declarative directives	*You have to be the duck.*
Mitigated obliges	
Pretend directives	*Pretend the duck can't swim.*
Question directives	*Could you put the duck on the lake?*
Joint directives	*You be the duck and I'll be the turtle.*
	Let's make the duck swim through here.
Tag questions	*The duck looks good there, doesn't it?*
State questions	*Do you want to play the duck?*
	Do you like the duck?
Permission questions	*Can I have the duck?*
Other obliges	
Attentional devices	*Lookit!*
	Jessica!
	Know what?
Informational questions	*Where's the duck?*

more than one category, it was assigned to the one judged to be more mitigated. Most of these cases involved the use of a tag question with at least one other mitigated form — for example, "Let's pretend we're going for a sail, okay?" This utterance could have been classified as a joint directive, a pretend directive, or a tag question. Because the tag question was considered the most mitigated of the three forms used, it was counted under that category.

All of the transcripts were coded by one experimenter; to assess coding reliability, a second experimenter independently coded 25% of the transcripts, randomly selected. Interrater agreement on the identification of pretend play utterances and obliges was 86.4% and 91.3%, respectively. Cohen's kappas for the oblige coding categories ranged from .79 to .98. The codes assigned by the first experimenter were used in all data analyses.

RESULTS

Data analysis focused on the pretend obliges produced by the 4-year-old target children; utterances produced by their siblings were not analyzed. Data from one child (a girl with an older sister) were excluded from the analysis because she produced no pretend utterances.

The 4-year-olds were chosen as the focus to facilitate comparison to past research on preschoolers' pretend play language and use of mitigation (e.g., Sachs, 1987; Leaper, 1991), which has primarily involved 4- and 5-year-olds. Because half of the 4-year-olds interacted with older siblings and half with younger siblings, focusing on them also made it possible to examine the effects of sibling status without confounding age differences.

Overall Amount of Talk

The children in the study averaged 267.1 total utterances in 30 minutes of taped interaction. On average, 134.4 utterances were classified as pretend utterances and 30.39 as pretend obliges. As shown in Table 2, boys and girls produced comparable numbers of total utterances, pretend utterances, and pretend obliges, regardless of whether they were observed with an older or a younger sibling. Separate 2 (gender) by 2 (sibling gender) by 2 (sibling status — older vs. younger) analyses of variance (ANOVAs) were performed for total utterances, pretend utterances, and pretend obliges; there were no significant main effects or interactions of gender, sibling gender, or sibling status.

There was, however, considerable variability across subjects in the

TABLE 2
Mean Utterances, Pretend Utterances, and Pretend Obliges Produced by Target Children

	Utterances	Pretend Utterances	Pretend Obliges
Girls			
With older siblings	242.1	146.0	26.4
	(102.7)[a]	(85.3)	(17.2)
With younger siblings	268.9	114.5	25.4
	(91.2)	(82.6)	(28.5)
Boys			
With older siblings	268.4	143.9	33.4
	(82.7)	(55.7)	(18.8)
With younger siblings	285.9	134.5	35.9
	(91.2)	(68.4)	(22.5)

[a]Figures in parentheses are standard deviations.

raw frequencies of utterances, pretend utterances, and pretend obliges. As a result, all subsequent analyses were based on arcsin-transformed percentages rather than absolute frequencies.

Unmitigated, Mitigated, and Other Obliges

When the children's use of mitigated and unmitigated obliges is considered across the board, the pattern of gender differences usually reported for peer interactions is not evident. Table 3 shows the rates of unmitigated, mitigated, and other obliges produced by the target children. A 2 (gender) by 2 (sibling status—older vs. younger) multivariate analysis of variance (MANOVA), with arcsin-transformed percentages of unmitigated, mitigated, and other obliges as the dependent variables, revealed no significant main effects or interactions for gender or sibling status. (The relatively small sample size made it impractical to include more than two factors in the MANOVA. Gender and sibling status were selected as the factors of primary interest; sibling gender was omitted. All subsequent MANOVAs follow the model described here.)

If anything, the trend in the children's use of obliges runs counter to the usually reported pattern of gender differences, although these differences were not statistically significant, due to high within-group variability and small sample size. Girls actually tended to use more unmitigated obliges than boys ($M = 21.6\%$ and 18.2%, respectively). Both boys and girls used unmitigated obliges more often than mitigated, particularly when interacting with younger siblings.

TABLE 3
Unmitigated, Mitigated, and Other Obliges Produced by Target Children
During Pretend Play[a]

	Unmitigated	Mitigated	Other
Girls			
With older siblings	46.6%	15.4%	39.5%
With younger siblings	57.3%	20.7%	22.0%
Boys			
With older siblings	31.3%	23.7%	45.1%
With younger siblings	46.9%	19.6%	33.6%

[a]Values represent mean percentages of pretend obliges.

Specific Categories of Obliges

Table 4 summarizes the rates of occurrence for the three specific types of unmitigated obliges. The overwhelming majority of unmitigated obliges produced by both boys and girls were simple imperatives. Prohibitions, including both negative imperatives ("Don't touch that!") and other utterances with clear prohibitive force ("Not the duck!"), were far less common. Declarative directives ("You have to put it this way") were almost nonexistent, except in girls' interactions with younger siblings.

A MANOVA with the three types of unmitigated obliges as the dependent variables yielded a significant main effect for sibling status ($F(3,25) = 3.49$, $p = .03$), but not for gender. Univariate analyses indicated a significant sibling status effect only for declarative directives ($F(1,27) = 7.99$, $p = .009$). Both boys and girls produced more declarative directives in interaction with younger siblings than in interaction with older siblings.

Table 5 summarizes the rates of occurrence for the six specific types of mitigated obliges. A MANOVA with the six types of mitigated obliges as the dependent variables yielded a significant main effect for sibling status ($F(6,22) = 3.86$, $p = .009$), but not for gender. Subsequent univariate analyses revealed a significant sibling status effect only for state questions ($F(1,27) = 5.85$, $p = .023$). Both boys and girls produced more state questions in interactions with younger siblings than in interactions with older siblings.

Although there was no overall multivariate effect of gender for mitigated obliges, there was a significant univariate effect of gender for

TABLE 4
Types of Unmitigated Obliges Produced by Target Children During Pretend Play[a]

	Imperatives	Prohibitions	Declarative Directives
Girls			
With older siblings	35.4%	9.1%	.7%
With younger siblings	42.8%	4.0%	10.5%
Boys			
With older siblings	27.6%	3.7%	—
With younger siblings	43.0%	1.9%	2.0%

[a]Values represent mean percentages of pretend obliges.

TABLE 5
Types of Mitigated Obliges Produced by Target Children During Pretend Play[a]

	Pretend Directives	Question Directives	Joint Directives	Tag Questions	State Questions	Permission Questions
Girls						
With older siblings	3.1%	—	1.5%	5.3%	0.8%	2.6%
With younger siblings	0.1%	1.6%	8.5%	6.6%	2.9%	1.0%
Boys						
With older siblings	4.0%	1.2%	7.9%	1.8%	0.4%	8.3%
With younger siblings	0.7%	0.9%	10.0%	1.6%	3.9%	2.6%

[a]Values represent mean percentages of pretend obliges.

tag questions ($F(1,27) = 4.80$, $p = .037$). In the absence of a multivariate effect, a single univariate effect is generally ignored. However, in this case there are three reasons for taking note of this result. First, the statistical power of the MANOVA used here is quite low, due to the small number of subjects per cell (8) and the relatively large number of dependent variables (6). Second, there is no particular reason to expect an overall effect of gender across all mitigated forms; however, there is reason to expect that certain specific forms might be used to a different extent by boys and by girls. Finally, a gender difference in use of tag questions has been widely reported for both children and adults, with girls and women showing a greater tendency to use this construction than boys and men.

Table 6 summarizes the rates of occurrence for the two specific types of other obliges. Informational questions were far more prevalent than attentional devices for both boys and girls. A MANOVA with the

TABLE 6
Types of Other Obliges Produced by Target Children During Pretend Play[a]

	Attentional Devices	Information Questions
Girls		
With older siblings	3.8%	30.8%
With younger siblings	4.5%	17.5%
Boys		
With older siblings	12.7%	32.4%
With younger siblings	7.0%	26.6%

[a]Values represent mean percentages of pretend obliges.

two types of other obliges as the dependent variables yielded no significant main effects or interactions for gender or sibling status.

DISCUSSION

Children's use of mitigated and unmitigated forms with siblings is not the same as that reported for peers, suggesting that the use of these forms is sensitive to the differing social contexts provided by the two relationships. In particular, girls in the present study used unmitigated forms at a much higher rate than Sachs (1987) reported for girls' peer interactions, and both boys and girls used mitigated forms at a much lower rate than Sachs found. Boys' and girls' use of unmitigated forms was roughly comparable to the rate Sachs reported for boys' use of these forms with peers. Apparently, in interacting with siblings, 4-year-olds of both sexes find it generally unnecessary to mitigate their directives and requests. However, it is interesting that the use of unmitigated forms is not much higher than the level previously reported for boys' peer interactions.

In contrast to the Sachs study, boys in the present study did not use imperatives or prohibitions more often than girls, and girls did not use joint directives and pretend directives more often than boys. For both boys and girls, the level of imperative use was higher in the present study than in the Sachs study, perhaps reflecting children's greater willingness to order their siblings around. In contrast, the level of use of joint directives and pretend directives was much lower than in the Sachs study; both of these forms can be used to express solidarity and cooperation, which may be sought more in relationships with peers than in relationships with siblings.

Sibling status emerged as a more significant variable than gender in children's use of mitigation with their siblings. However, it was not the case that children used more mitigated forms across the board with older siblings or more unmitigated forms with younger siblings. Instead, particular forms were addressed more frequently to younger siblings than to older siblings.

One of the forms that children were more likely to address to younger siblings was the declarative directive. Although this form is categorized as an unmitigated oblige, it appeared to be used in different circumstances and perhaps for different purposes than simple imperatives ("Do X.") and prohibitions ("Don't do X.") were. Children used imperatives and prohibitions at generally comparable rates with both older and younger siblings; in contrast, declarative directives were used almost exclusively in dealing with younger siblings. In many situations, this form is a more emphatic way of requesting compliance than a simple imperative would be. It may be a way of asserting one's power to an unwilling and perhaps skeptical younger sibling; it often followed other attempts to direct a younger sibling's behavior, as in the following example:

> ((*Younger brother is using toy crane to unload box from*
> *toy train*))
> Older sister: Marky, leave it on here.
> ((*No response; younger brother continues to operate crane*))
> Older sister: Mark!
> ((*Still no response*))
> (5.0)
> Older sister: You have to leave it on here now.

The other form that was directed primarily to younger siblings was the state question. State questions are categorized as a mitigated form; when directed to a younger sibling, they generally served a cajoling function. They seemed to reflect not genuine concern with a sibling's feelings or desires, but instead attempts to impose an older child's will, as in the following examples:

> ((*Younger brother takes train off tracks*))
> Older sister: You keep it on the train tracks. Keep it on here.
> (5.0)
> ((*Older sister takes train, starts putting it back on tracks*))
> Older sister: That's where it, where we want it. Cause that's the
> train tracks. Do you like the train tracks?

> ((*Younger sister trying to put village church together*))
> Older brother: Is that how the church goes?
> Younger sister: Huh-uh.
> Older brother: Do you wanta see how it goes?
> Younger sister: Uh-huh.
> Older brother: See? ((*Takes pieces, starts putting church*
>   *together*))

The absence of significant gender effects in the present study may be due partly to the relatively small sample size and resulting low statistical power of the analyses. As noted in the Results section, one particular mitigated form that was used more often by girls than by boys was the tag question. Although this gender difference would usually be ignored because of the lack of an overall multivariate effect of gender for mitigated forms, a closer examination of tag questions in the present transcripts reveals some interesting differences in usage patterns by girls and by boys. Girls used tag questions especially often with older brothers (9.4% of all pretend obliges) and younger sisters (12.1% of all pretend obliges). These two concentrations of tag question use represent different ways of using mitigation in asymmetrical relationships. In conversations with older brothers, girls used tag questions to seek confirmation of facts or permission for an intended action, as these examples from two different sibling pairs illustrate:

| Younger sister: | These little things are mailboxes, right, Charlie? ((*Holding up mailboxes for older brother's inspection*)) |
| Older brother: | Yeah. |

Younger sister:	This is a little girl, isn't it? ((*Holding up little girl figure*))
Older brother:	Yeah.
Younger sister:	That's me. Okay, I'm looking for a little boy. (5.0)
Younger sister:	I'll just use a little girl for a little boy, okay?

In conversations with younger sisters, girls used tag questions to engage the younger child or soften an action already taken.

| Younger sister: | Look. ((*Holds black dog figure out to older sister*)) |
| Older sister: | That's a big black dog, isn't it, Jessie? |

((*Older sister adds piece to younger sister's train*))
| Older sister: | You can have this on your train, okay? |
| Younger sister: | Okay. |

Girls occasionally used tag questions along with joint directives or pretend directives to produce a doubly or triply mitigated utterance, as in the following examples: "Let's pretend this is a lake, okay?" or "Sean, pretend that's, pretend that's both, okay?" Only one boy produced an utterance of this type.

The results of this study support the idea that gender-distinctive patterns of language use are sensitive to variations in situation and interaction partner. In particular, the social demands of sibling and peer relationships elicit different patterns of mitigated and unmitigated conversational forms during pretend play, and gender differences in the use of mitigation do not seem to carry over from peer interactions to sibling interactions. Both of these conclusions support Maccoby's notion that gender-distinctive behavior occurs in the context of particular social interactions and relationships and should not be treated as a cross-situational individual trait.

REFERENCES

Austin, A. M. B., Salehi, M., & Leffler, A. (1987). Gender and developmental differences in children's conversations. *Sex Roles, 16,* 497–510.

Black, B. & Hazen, N. L. (1990). Social status and patterns of communication in acquainted and unacquainted preschool children. *Developmental Psychology, 26,* 379–387.

Blank, M., & Franklin, E. (1980). Dialogue with preschoolers: A cognitively-based system of assessment. *Applied Psycholinguistics, 1,* 127–150.

Brim, O. J. (1958). Family structure and sex role learning by children: A further analysis of Helen Koch's data. *Sociometry, 21,* 1–16.

DeHart, G. (1990). Young children's linguistic interaction with mothers and siblings. Doctoral dissertation, University of Minnesota, 1990. *Dissertation Abstracts International, 51,* 3156B.

DeHart, G., Laliberte, J., Strazza, H., Shanahan, E., Shiledar Baxi, B., Mulcock, E., & Keogh, J. (1994, April). *Parents' perceptions of preschoolers' sibling relationships.* Poster presented at the Conference on Human Development, Pittsburgh, PA.

Dunn, J. (1988). *The beginnings of social understanding.* Cambridge, MA: Harvard University Press.

Dunn, J., & Kendrick C. (1982). *Siblings: Love, envy, and understanding.* Cambridge, MA: Harvard University Press.

Hinde, R. A. (1979). *Towards understanding relationships.* New York: Academic.

Hoff-Ginsberg, E. (1991). Mother–child conversation in different social classes and communicative settings. *Child Development, 62,* 782–796.

Leaper, C. (1991). Influence and involvement in children's discourse: Age, gender, and partner effects. *Child Development, 62,* 797–811.

Maccoby, E. E. (1990). Gender and relationships: A developmental account. *American Psychologist, 45,* 513–520.

Maccoby, E. E., & Jacklin, C. N. (1987). Gender segregation in childhood. In E. H. Reese (Ed.), *Advances in child development and behavior* (Vol. 20, pp. 239–287). New York: Academic.

Sachs, J. (1987). Preschool boys' and girls' language use in pretend play. In S. U. Philips, S. Steele, & C. Tanz (Eds.), *Language, gender, and sex in comparative perspective* (pp. 178–188). Cambridge, England: Cambridge University Press.

Sheldon, A. (1990). Pickle fights: Gendered talk in preschool disputes. *Discourse Processes, 13,* 5–31.

Sheldon, A. (1992). Conflict talk: Sociolinguistic challenges to self-assertion and how young girls meet them. *Merrill-Palmer Quarterly, 38,* 95–117.

Stoneman, Z., Brody, G. H., & MacKinnon, C. E. (1986). Same-sex and cross-sex siblings: Activity choices, roles, behavior, and gender stereotypes. *Sex Roles, 15,* 495–511.

Tannen, D. (1993). The relativity of language strategies: Rethinking power and solidarity in gender and dominance. In D. Tannen (Ed.), *Gender and conversational interaction* (pp. 165–188). New York: Oxford University Press.

Thorne, B. (1986). Girls and boys together, but mostly apart. In W. W. Hartup & Z. Rubin (Eds.), *Relationships and development* (pp. 167–184). Hillsdale, NJ: Lawrence Erlbaum Associates, Inc.

Subscription Order Form

Please ❑ enter ❑ renew my subscription to

RESEARCH ON LANGUAGE AND SOCIAL INTERACTION
Volume 29, 1996, Quarterly

Subscription prices per volume:

Individual: ❑ $30.00 (US/Canada) ❑ $60.00 (All Other Countries)

Institution: ❑ $160.00 (US/Canada) ❑ $190.00 (All Other Countries)

Subscriptions are entered on a calendar-year basis only and must be prepaid in US currency -- check, money order, or credit card. **Offer expires 12/31/96. NOTE: Institutions must pay institutional rates.** Any institution paying for an individual subscription will be invoiced for the balance of the institutional subscription rate.

❑ Payment Enclosed

Total Amount Enclosed $_____

❑ Charge My Credit Card

❑ VISA ❑ MasterCard ❑ AMEX ❑ Discover

Exp. Date_____

Card Number _____

Signature _____
(Credit card orders cannot be processed without your signature.)

Please print clearly to ensure proper delivery.

Name _____

Address _____

_____

City _____ State _____ Zip+4 _____
Prices are subject to change without notice.

Lawrence Erlbaum Associates, Inc.
Journal Subscription Department
10 Industrial Avenue, Mahwah, NJ 07430
(201) 236-9500 FAX (201) 236-0072

THE TALK OF THE CLINIC
Explorations in the Analysis of Medical and Therapeutic Discourse
edited by
G. H. Morris
Texas Tech University
Ronald J. Chenail
Nova Southeastern University

A VOLUME IN LEA's COMMUNICATION SERIES

This collection of original papers by scholars who closely analyze the talk of the clinic features studies that were conceived with the aim of contributing to clinical practitioners' insight about how their talk works. No previous communication text has attempted to take such a practitioner-sensitive posture with its research presentations. Each chapter focuses on one or more performances that clinical practitioners -- in consort with their clients or colleagues -- must achieve with some regularity. These speech acts are consequential for effective practice and sometimes present themselves as problematic.

Rather than calling for research to be simplified or reoriented in order for practitioners to understand it, these authors interpret state-of-the-art descriptive analysis for its practical import for clinicians. Each contributor delves deeply into clinical practice and its wisdom; therefore, each is positioned to identify alternative clinical practices and techniques and to appreciate practitioners' means of performing effectively. When reflective practitioners encounter these new pieces of work, productive alterations in how their work is done can be stimulated. By reading this work, reflective practitioners will now have new ways of considering their talk and new possibilities for speaking effectively.

The volume is uniquely constructed so as to engage in dialogue with these reflective practitioners as they struggle to articulate their work. A practical wisdom-as-research trend has recently emerged in the clinical fields stimulating these practitioners to explore new and more informative ways -- communication and literary theory, ethnography, and discourse analysis -- to express what they do in clinics and hospitals. With the studies presented in this book, the editors build upon this dialectical process between practitioner and researcher, thus helping this productive conversation to continue.

0-8058-1372-1 [cloth] / 1995 / 344pp. / $79.95
0-8058-1373-X [paper] / 1995 / 344pp. / $29.95

Prices subject to change without notice.

Lawrence Erlbaum Associates, Inc.
10 Industrial Avenue, Mahwah, NJ 07430
201/236-9500   FAX 201/236-0072

Call toll-free to order: 1-800-9-BOOKS-9...9am to 5pm EST only.
e-mail to: orders@leahq.mhs.compuserve.com
visit LEA's web site at http://www.erlbaum.com

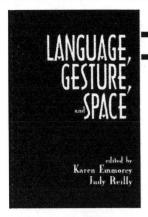

LANGUAGE, GESTURE, AND SPACE

edited by
Karen Emmorey
The Salk Institute for Biological Studies
Judy Snitzer Reilly
San Diego State University

This book brings together papers which address a range of issues regarding the nature and structure of sign languages and other gestural systems, and how they exploit the space in which they are conveyed. The chapters focus on five pertinent areas reflecting different, but related research topics: space in language and gesture; point of view and referential shift; morphosyntax of verbs in ASL; gestural systems and sign language; and language acquisition and gesture.

Sign languages and gestural systems are produced in physical space; they manipulate spatial contrasts for linguistic and communicative purposes. In addition to exploring the different functions of space, researchers discuss similarities and differences between visual-gestural systems — established sign languages, pidgin sign language (International Sign), "homesign" systems developed by deaf children with no sign language input, novel gesture systems invented by hearing nonsigners, and the gesticulation that accompanies speech. The development of gesture and sign language in children is also examined in both hearing and deaf children, charting the emergence of gesture ("manual babbling"), its use as a prelinguistic communicative device, and its transformation into language-like systems in homesigners. Finally, theoretical linguistic accounts of the structure of sign languages are provided in chapters dealing with the analysis of referential shift, the structure of narrative, the analysis of tense and the structure of the verb phrase in American Sign Language. Taken together, the chapters in this volume present a comprehensive picture of sign language and gesture research from a group of international scholars who investigate a range of communicative systems from formal sign languages to the gesticulation that accompanies speech.

0-8058-1378-0 [cloth] / 1995 / 464pp. / $79.95
Special Prepaid Offer! $39.95
No further discounts apply.
Prices subject to
change without notice.

Lawrence Erlbaum Associates, Inc.
LEA 10 Industrial Ave., Mahwah, NJ 07430
201/236-9500   FAX 201/236-0072

Call toll-free to order: 1-800-9-BOOKS-9...9am to 5pm EST only.
e-mail to: orders@leahq.mhs.compuserve.com
visit LEA's web site at http://www.erlbaum.com

THE CONSEQUENTIALITY OF COMMUNICATION

Edited by
Stuart J. Sigman
SUNY, University at Albany
A Volume in LEA's Communication Series

In a bold attempt to redirect the ways theories of communication are conceived and research on communication processes are conducted, this volume questions prevailing communication scholarship, which emphasizes the cultural, psychological, and sociological variables that impact on and/or are impacted by communication. Instead of focusing on the consequences of communication, this books urges readers to examine the consequentiality of communication -- what it is about the communication process that enables it to play a defining role in our lives. Communication is not a neutral conveyor of meanings derived from culture, cognition, or social structure, and is not explained by correlations with external variables. Meaning emerges from the communication process itself; it is dependent upon what transpires during the real-time moments of communicators behaving with each other. To properly study this new paradigm, a new vocabulary for thinking about the consequentiality of communication is needed and proposed.

Four theoretical orientations are used to stake out this new territory: coordinated management of meaning, neo-rhetorical theory, conversation analysis, and social communication theory. While there are points of agreement and overlap on the need to study communication as inherently consequential, there are also differences across the four theories -- in the value of "rules" as an explanatory concept, on the relationship between structure and process, and on the very constitution of a "theory." Thus, this book has the benefit of articulating a new paradigm for communication scholarship without losing sight of the discipline's rich diversity.

0-8058-1269-5 [cloth] / 1995 / 264pp. / $59.95
0-8058-1765-4 [paper] / 1995 / 264pp. / $22.50

Lawrence Erlbaum Associates, Inc.

Prices subject to
change without notice.

10 Industrial Avenue, Mahwah, NJ 07430
201/236-9500   FAX 201/236-0072

Call toll-free to order: 1-800-9-BOOKS-9...9am to 5pm EST only.
e-mail to: orders@leahq.mhs.compuserve.com
visit LEA's web site at http://www.erlbaum.com

LEA

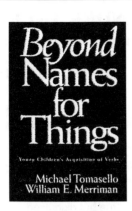

GENDER TALES
Tensions in the Schools
edited by
Judith S. Kleinfeld
University of Alaska, Fairbanks
Suzanne Yerian
University of Washington

A book of "real world" cases, this text introduces "flashpoint" issues related to gender equity in the schools. It immerses readers in the human dilemmas teachers face when they set out to provide equal opportunities for -- and to develop the abilities of -- all of their students. Each case, a true but disguised situation, presents the pedagogical concerns, ethical questions, competing values, and complexity of social change teachers face on a daily basis in their classrooms. These cases help readers to identify and understand ideas and issues by relating them to both their own and others' real-life experiences. The book includes activities and discussion questions to involve readers in critical thinking about the issues raised in the cases and in applying this knowledge to their own current or future classroom practice.

Using a casebook approach, the text is organized in five sections. Designed to help readers grapple with the issues raised by contextualizing them in stories that are authentic and engaging, it emphasizes the teacher's role as a skilled professional who thinks critically and makes decisions, and creates lively and involved class discussion by making room for students with diverse perspectives.

Contents: Dedication. Preface. Acknowledgments. **Part I:** *The Meaning of Gender Equality in the Schools.* Introduction. **B. Weikel,** "Girlspeak" and "Boyspeak": Gender Differences in Classroom Discussion. **J. Skolnick,** A Rare Commodity. **D. Reynolds,** The Teacher Who Knew Too Much. **S. Yerian,** Jane, the Reluctant Mathlete. **S. Wassermann,** Her Work Is Not Scholarly! **J.S. Kleinfeld,** Girls on the Wrestling Team: A Community Fight. **J.S. Kleinfeld,** The Venerable Tradition of Separate-Sex Schooling. **Part II:** *Increasing Achievement Among Young Women.* Introduction. **Gender Equity Project Teachers,** The Square Parachute: Science in Gender-mixed Groups. **B. McKinny,** Burn Schools to the Ground. **B. Weikel, S, Yerian,** Tough Anna. **R. Silverman, W. M. Welty, S. Lyon,** Diane News: The Choice. *Case Studies for Teacher Problem Solving.* **J. Shulman, A. Mesa-Bains,** Opening Pandora's Box: The Mystery Behind an "Ideal Student." *eds., Diversity in the Classroom,* **R. Kleinfeld,** Going to the Oracle: Susan Consults the "Big Feminist." **S. Yerian, B. Weikel,** You'll Be Washing Dishes. **Part III:** *Establishing Professional Standing for Female Teachers.* Introduction. **J. Skolnick,** Diane: Gender, Culture, and a Crisis of Classroom Control. **Gender Equity Project Teachers,** Patsy: The Hunt for the Golden Egg. **A. Hansen,** The Day the Heat Went On, from **Harvard Business School Case Series. Gender Equity Project Teachers,** The Alliance. **Part IV:** *Sexual Harassment in the Schools.* Introduction. **J.S. Kleinfeld,** The Boys on the Bus: Bad Language or Sexual Harassment? **E Miller,** Lisa's Complaint. **S.S. Wineburg,** When Good Intentions Aren't Enough. **T. Bliss,** *Who Is the Victim?* **Part V:** *Sexual Slurs, Sexual Stereotyping, and the Marketplace of Ideas.* Introduction. **P. Finley,** "T" Is for T-shirt...and Take It to Court. **I. Macneil,** *Jockeying for Position: The Battle over Classroom Speech.* **J. Martin,** *The Girls at Central — They Sure Got Nice Behinds.* **P. Hutchings,** *March in Minneapolis.* About the Editors.
0-8058-8010-0 [paper only] / 1995 / 224pp. / $19.00
0-8058-8011-9 [Instructor's Manual] / 1995 / Free upon adoption
Previously published by St. Martin's Press.

Lawrence Erlbaum Associates, Inc.

Prices subject to
change without notice.

10 Industrial Avenue, Mahwah, NJ 07430
201/236-9500   FAX 201/236-0072

Call toll-free to order: 1-800-9-BOOKS-9...9am to 5pm EST only.
e-mail to: orders@leahq.mhs.compuserve.com
visit LEA's web site at http://www.erlbaum.com

LEA